Travelling
to the
Edge of the World

KATHLEEN JONES

The Book Mill

Other Books By Kathleen Jones

<u>Biography</u>
Margaret Cavendish: A Glorious Fame, the Life of the   Duchess of Newcastle, Bloomsbury Publishing & The Book Mill
Christina Rossetti: Learning not to be First, Oxford University Press & The Book Mill
A Passionate Sisterhood: The Sisters, Wives and Daughter of the Lake Poets, Virago & The Book Mill
Catherine Cookson: The Biography, Times Warner
Seeking Catherine Cookson's Da, Constable Robinson
Katherine Mansfield: The Storyteller, Penguin NZ, Edinburgh University Press
Margaret Forster: A Life in Books, The Book Mill
Norman Nicholson: The Whispering Poet, The Book Mill

<u>Fiction</u>
Three and Other Stories, The Book Mill
The Sun's Companion, The Book Mill
The Centauress, The Book Mill

<u>Poetry</u>
Unwritten Lives, Redbeck Press
Not Saying Goodbye at Gate 21, Templar Poetry

<u>Anthology</u>
Other People's Lives, The Book Mill

<u>As Kate Gordon</u>
Published by Constable Robinson
An Alternative Guide to Weddings
An Alternative Guide to Baptism and Baby-naming
An Alternative Guide to Funerals

The Book Mill
www.thebookmill.co.uk
The Book Mill is an imprint of Ferber Jones Ltd

Printed by CreateSpace

Acknowledgements

First of all I would like to thank the Wild Women of Moniakh Mhor (you know who you are) who helped to nurture the idea for this book. My life partner and editor, Neil Ferber, has also been essential to its development. Thanks also to Sharon Blackie and David Knowles for their encouragement and for publishing some of my 'Haida Gwaii' poems in their magazine *Earthlines* and the Two Ravens Press anthology *Entanglements*. To all the people of British Columbia and Haida Gwaii who made me so welcome, talked to me, gave me hospitality, and answered my many, many questions, I owe a huge debt. Particular thanks to Barbara, Katie and Bill, Rachael, Rachel, Reg, Jennifer, Susan, James, Lisa, Sherry, Barnaby, James, and the owners and staff of the Copper Beech and Haida House guesthouses. Names have been changed to protect the privacy and identity of many of the people who helped me so generously. Thanks also to the Royal Literary Fund, because without their financial help, I wouldn't have been able to visit British Columbia. All the photographs in this book, unless otherwise attributed, are copyright to the author and may not be reproduced without permission. For the other images, every effort has been made to trace the owners and the author would be very happy to be contacted by anyone who could not be found. No reply was ever received from the Cultural Committee of the Haida Nation, so I can only assume that the nature of this book did not infringe any ethical standards.

Contents

1. The Kick

2. Vancouver

3. Art or Anthropology?

4. Emily Carr and The Parade of Ships

5. The Schools of Sorrow

6. Alert Bay

7. The Legend of Siwidis

8. Beside the Singing Forest

9. Port McNeill – Billy and Jean-Paul

10. In Margaret Atwood's Bedroom.

11. Two Massets

12. An Appointment with an Eagle

13. The Edge of the World

14. The Spirit in the Blood

15. Skidegate

16. The Great Dying

17. An Encounter with a Bear

18. The Bank Robber's Wife

19. Everything is Connected

Travelling to the Edge of the World

'Where your world ends, ours begins.'
Haida saying

For months I'd been feeling depressed, anxious and powerless. There seemed to be no solution to the perfect storm of economic and environmental chaos that was (and still is) approaching. My own personal life felt just as stormy and unsolvable. But at the moment when I felt most depressed, I read a book by an American poet called Robert Bringhurst. It was called *A Story as Sharp as a Knife*. At first what drew me to the book was the discussion about narrative. I'm a writer, and I'm fascinated by narrative. Storytelling is fundamental to the human psyche, even our brains are structured to construct narratives. Every time we access a memory, our brain re-assembles its components as a story, making it slightly different every time.

Bringhurst was writing about a First Nation people called the Haida, who live on remote islands off the coasts of British Columbia and Alaska, on the eastern edge of the Pacific Ocean. Over a hundred years ago their oral literary tradition, which had been developing for nearly ten thousand years, was transcribed by an anthropologist. Most of the stories, told as poems, had never been translated until Bringhurst began to study them. The way the Haida structured their poems and stories was quite different from the literary traditions we have here in the west and that fascinated me. Here was a tradition as old as the Greeks, but offering a different model to follow.

They also had a mythology which was not simply about a group of humans who were actually gods in disguise, but which was animist in origin – regarding animals as supernatural beings and placing humans firmly within the world's ecology as a cog in the works, rather than superior beings who were in charge of it all. 'Everything is connected to everything', was one of the Haida sayings and it summed up their philosophy. For their world to function, there had to be a balance in all things. This was reflected in their literature too; their literary forms involved a balancing of themes and events. I read all the translations I could source and everything I could find out about the Haida.

Here, it seemed, was a people who knew how to live in the world without harming it. Perhaps they had an answer to the ills of the twenty first century. Perhaps they could teach us how to live without destroying the planet that supports us. I knew that somehow I had to get there.

1. The Kick

'Wild is a word like "soul". Such a thing may not exist, but we want it, and we know what we mean when we talk about it.'
Kathleen Jamie

The sun is shining as I leave Cumbria in mid-May. The trees are just coming into leaf and there are lambs in the fields. The Lakeland fells on one side and the Pennines on the other, have shadings of white where wintry showers have fallen overnight. Big puffs of cloud are being driven across the blue sky by a cold north-westerly wind. It's as good a leave-taking as you get. From the train I can see the stone walls that divide the landscape, marking out old fields scattered with erratic boulders left behind by ice age glaciers. I wonder what it will all look like in four weeks time when I come back.

If I come back.

The thought stops my breath for a moment. So many things can happen. I always have these moments of anxiety when I go away. Travelling is a risk and going alone even more so, but sometimes it's the only way to travel. That I intend to come back is never in doubt. As a third generation immigrant to northern England, I feel that, if I belong anywhere, it's here. Although I've lived all over the world at various times in my life, I've always felt myself in exile when living anywhere other than Cumbria. But, sometimes it seems as though I was born to be a nomad. There's an English nursery rhyme that predicts your future according to the day on which you were born, in lines that were often quoted to me when I was a child.

Wednesday's child is full of woe,
Thursday's child has far to go.

I was born on a Thursday in a small farm-worker's cottage in a hamlet too small to be visible on a map. Eden is on my birth certificate; the Eden river valley, a small paradise in a wild landscape. When I was three my father moved us up to the Scottish borders to live on a croft in a place so wild there was no road to it. The front and back doors opened straight out onto the fellside and cows and horses were stabled next to the living accommodation. There was no electricity or telephone, water came from a spring and the only toilet was an earth closet.

A family picnic at the croft, Bewcastle

My parents were 'off-comers' — my mother a land girl displaced by the war; my father the child of an Irish immigrant family, mill workers, cattle drovers and small farmers, displaced by poverty. He loved the land, loved farming, but couldn't afford to buy his own farm, so he laboured for another land owner in return for the croft. The people who wrenched a living from the land around us belonged to that land as my parents never could. They all traced their ancestry back a thousand years to the Vikings who had settled there. Our neighbours never used their surnames but were known by their holdings; Willy the Crewe, Bobby the Row, Maggie the Inskip. The landscape was named in Norse. A river valley was a Wath or a Syke, streams were Becks, hills were

11

Fells, and the small strip of tree shelter behind the house was a Garth. The dialect spoken by everyone looked towards Oslo rather than London. It was a strong language, with few passive verbs or feminine word endings; if you were busy you were 'thrang', talk was 'crack'. It was muscular on the tongue and picturesque on the ear. The Queen's English spoken at home or at school seemed colourless by comparison.

Most people over fifty had never been further than the nearest small town in their entire lives and many of them could read or write little more than their names. Having no electricity, there was no television to fill the evenings. People walked to each other's houses and had 'good crack'. As they talked, they peopled the landscape around me with stories. Old Sworley who had hanged himself in the barn believing that he had killed his wife by pitching her down the well (in fact she'd managed to climb out and run off to the town). The woman whose ghost was supposed to walk the track on winter nights, where her children had been lost in a snow storm. How people had burned their furniture to keep warm through the winter of '47. How Billy the Hope had spent three days floundering through the snow with a horse and sled to fetch the supplies for his starving family. His story, as they told it, was a tale worthy of a Greek epic.

And on those fireside nights I learned my own family stories, as I listened to my father and grandfather talking about ancestors who went across the sea on sailing ships to bring back cargos of bananas and marry exotic women; of others who drove herds of cattle from Ireland to London, or despaired over errant children, disinherited their offspring and fought bitterly over religion. These were stories they had learned from their own grandparents. I was aware, even at nine or ten, that I was listening to an unbroken memory line going back two hundred years — stories passing like heirlooms from one generation to another. The tellers seemed to know exactly what great-great-grandmother Bridie had said to her daughter Frances Theresa when she came home with a baby she wasn't supposed to have, fathered by a footman at the house where she was in service. The fine rooms, the uniforms, the very porcelain crockery she washed in a lead lined sink were all there in the story, leaping like a hologram in the firelight before my eyes. The account of my great-great-uncle Edward who had stood preaching the gospel of temperance outside his father's pub on a Tyneside quay, was pure Catherine Cookson. It was hardly surprising that I grew up with a love of history, language and narrative that was somehow equated with the wild, untamed landscape beyond the kitchen door.

Now, I live on the banks of the River Eden, not far upstream from the place where I was born, in an old mill perched on the edge of the river where it enters a natural gorge between sandstone cliffs. I can watch the river's variations through my window as I write, the delicate patterns of light and shade, the constant changes of mood. The murmur of the weir provides a continuing soundscape through every night and day. I know the riverbank intimately. When I wake in the morning I can watch herons disputing territory above the weir, red squirrels bolting across the footbridge, spawning salmon in the gravel beds. Once, on a deserted morning, a family of three otters walked along the foot of the weir, and once we surprised a bird of prey lifting a duckling off the water. The river is a source of continuing fascination and delight.

Looking across the River Eden to the mill

So why am I leaving my own little paradise to travel to the edge of the world? It all began with a growing disillusionment with Western politics and particularly with the West's attitude to environmental issues. There has, for a long time now, been a hollow, anxious feeling at the pit of my stomach. The news, both environmental, political and economic, makes me sad and frustrated because I care deeply about the state of the world we live in but I don't seem able to do anything about it. What will the future hold for my children, or my lovely grandchildren growing up so optimistically in a world that should be full of promise, but which now feels quite the opposite?

In the Mediterranean and the Andaman seas, refugees and asylum seekers are drowning in their thousands as they are turned away by affluent countries who could well afford to help. All over the world, big corporations are turning sections of the land and the ocean into wastelands that are too polluted to be safe. There are very few places in the world that man has not tampered with, and these days we do it by remote control, polluting an atmosphere and ocean that have no boundaries. The results are more than just environmental. Climate change and economic instability cause conflict. Some of the poorest countries are at war with each other, creating a living hell for the people who have to live there. In our own society, inequality is increasing at an alarming rate, fuelled by the Austerity measures adopted by our governments as an answer to the banking crisis. As one economist put it, the result has been that 'money is being transferred from the have-nots to the have-yachts'. Long-term this, too, can only lead to conflict.

Then, in the autumn of 2014, I flew to Singapore and was horrified to be greeted at the airport by a notice exhorting all pregnant women, the elderly and people with breathing difficulties to stay inside with their windows and doors tightly shut because air pollution had reached a critical level. The city was hidden under a brown smog. You could see across the street, but only just. I thought that at least this must be some kind of environmental crisis, but no, people told me, this happens often. You have to stay inside. If you go outside you'd better wear a mask. Everyone behaved as if this was quite normal and I found it unsettling.

14

Singapore is supposed to be one of the cleanest cities in Asia and it's situated on the coast where sea breezes should keep the air fresh. What had gone wrong? Singapore, like most big cities, especially in hot countries, has a high level of pollution from cars and industrial activity. Also, like most big cities, it shares the air it breathes with its neighbours. The slashing and burning of the rainforest in Indonesia sends clouds of thick smoke across the country when the wind is in the right direction. It's estimated that more than three thousand square miles of forest was destroyed in Indonesia last year.

China has one of the highest pollution records of any country. In its biggest cities the air is so polluted it is carcinogenic and people cycle round the streets in masks. The death rate from respiratory diseases is significant. But nowhere in Singapore, or China, have I seen anyone standing in the street with a placard protesting that the air they need to breathe to keep them alive is being poisoned. People shrug their shoulders, accept it as a fact of life and put on a mask. Why are we so accepting of something so unacceptable? Why aren't people on the streets in their tens of thousands demanding that their governments do something so that their most basic need can be met. Clean air to breathe. You don't breathe; you don't live. It's that simple.

But it isn't. In a modern economy, people have to work to live and, just as they risked life and limb in Victorian factories and sweat shops, people put up with the consequences of their employment because it puts bread on the table and allows them to buy the clothes on their backs and the cars in their garages. They are part of a self-perpetuating cycle they can't get out of. The production of goods, power, drugs and chemicals that is required in our daily lives is damaging our environment, yet we seem unable to see a way out of the loop because we need the employment they provide in order to live and we want the goods that are produced. In the war between the environment and economics, economics definitely seems to be winning out.

But that situation, bad as it is, wasn't the whole story behind my depression. I write for a living and inside myself there was a creative restlessness and dissatisfaction with an increasingly stale

European literary tradition. Everything in poetry and prose seemed to have already been written. My connection with the natural world around me seemed also to have been broken. The girl who had run barefoot on the open fells among the larks and the curlews had vanished and the spontaneous joy she felt at being part of this wild landscape had long since been crushed under tax returns, publishers' deadlines, student reports, blog posts and bank statements. I felt flat, exhausted, despairing and powerless.

Then, at my lowest moment, I found a book by a Canadian poet, Robert Bringhurst, called A Story as Sharp as a Knife. It told the story of a group of First Nation people who inhabited remote islands off the northern coast of British Columbia and had a literary and artistic tradition reaching back more than ten thousand years. Their world view was, like most First Nation traditions, holistic, seeing human beings as part of the whole cycle of life on earth, part of an organism, a fragile ecosystem that commanded the utmost respect. Their world, which emerged after a great flood, was pulled up out of the water by the Raven, who discovered human beings hiding in a giant clam shell and, thinking that he could have some fun with them, tempted them out. The more I read of their myths and legends, the more I wanted to go. I dreamed of standing on North Beach, a spit of land where you can look straight out across the Pacific, where the Raven found the clam shell. I wanted to go somewhere truly wild, where the echoes of some of those first narratives still lingered.

But I was also aware that there was a darker side to their history. The Haida people were, like many of the First Nation people of North America, the victims of an unacknowledged colonial genocide.1 Before 1860 more than twenty thousand people lived on these islands, as hunter-gatherers, with a cultural tradition stretching back more than ten thousand years. Within two decades of European colonisation the population had been reduced to around five hundred and their way of life had become unsustainable. Between the saw mills and the fish canneries and the missionary stations, the Haida tried to keep some remnants of their culture intact. Their children were taken away from them to be sent to residential schools where (apart from suffering appalling abuse) they were forbidden to speak their own language. Haida traditions went underground and soon only the old people remembered which families belonged to the Raven or the Eagle clans, and the significance of the stories that had been handed on from generation to generation was sometimes lost.

Dispossession was almost complete. The British Columbian Commissioner for Land remarked at the end of the nineteenth century that the Haida had no claim to their land because 'they can put no value on it and it has no utility for them'. Because they did not exploit or cultivate it, and because land ownership was a totally alien concept (how can you 'own' something that existed millions of years before you did?) their land rights were taken away to be given to 'some industrious people' ie colonial immigrants. The Indian Act of 1876 left the native people of British Columbia very little and gave them the legal status of children. It was the ultimate act of dispossession and repression, and it has never been repealed.

But the Haida stayed and they remembered, and eventually they fought back with lawyers and high court writs, and now the 'Queen Charlotte Islands' are once more Haida Gwaii, home to the Haida Nation.

The old women who were still native Haida speakers, passed on the language and the traditions. One small boy, who slept with his grandmother, Old Nanaay, remembered waking up and watching her getting dressed, surprised to see her body covered in tattoos across her chest and down her arms. "What are they, Grandma?" he asked. "Boy, that's who you are," she replied. Her tattoos told the story of her clan relationships, like the carved poles still rotting in the forests where the ruined Haida houses had been swallowed up by new growth. But she was one of the last of her generation to wear 'the marks of her lineage' on her body.[2]

So that is why I'm on a plane, at 38,000 feet, enduring all the discomforts of long-haul travel to visit a group of islands off the north western coast of British Columbia and Alaska called Haida Gwaii. I don't know what will happen, or what difference it will make to my life; I just know that I have to do it.

2. Vancouver

'The fundamental basis of any society is its relationship to nature.'
The Ecologist, 'Exposing Technocracy', June 28th 2015

My carbon footprint is enormous and quite unjustifiable. But with a partner in Italy and children in New Zealand, Cambodia and Cuba, as well as travel for my work, it seems an insoluble problem. It's a great irony that the people who are most concerned about their impact on the planet's ecosystems seem to need to travel to get their message across.

There's no solution, until someone invents zero carbon transport, except to go back to the days of sailing ships and horse power. Ships and wagons were made from renewable timber, not polluting plastics, precious metals and finite resources. They were propelled by animals and the elements, not by the blood of ancient swamps, exhaled as poison into the planet's atmosphere. There are times when I think that human beings are one of the least intelligent species on the planet, if we can't see what we've done to it and acknowledge the consequences. We even know how to solve the problems we've created, but we don't act. It's hard to give things up, particularly things we enjoy.

I'm flying over the vast expanses of Northern Canada — Alberta and the Yukon — alternately black and white with spring blooms of ochre and just the suggestion of green, as well as lace-patterned ice crusts over frozen lakes and drifts of blown snow. From here it looks a wasteland, but I know it's not. This is one of the last great wildernesses, which we need to protect from fracking and the extraction of oil from tar sands — fossil fuel we don't need (Saudi Arabia and Russia have more than enough for all of us) and which we can never afford to burn if the world is to remain habitable.

Almost everyone on this aeroplane is over-weight (I include myself in this) and some are frankly obese. The number of relatively young people who were being given assistance to board, walking with sticks, was a shocking illustration of what an unhealthy society we have become. Seat belt extensions are in evidence everywhere. Watching an extremely obese passenger try to squeeze into a narrow toilet cubicle is painful. We are a culture of excess. We have been too successful at plundering natural resources for consumption. Out of the plane window, 38,000 feet below, on the frozen tundra, most of us would not survive because we lack the skills to produce or hunt our own food. We have become so reliant on a succession of middle-men to produce and process what we eat we no longer know where the food on the supermarket shelves has come from or how it got there.

Vancouver faces the Pacific ocean, but is shielded from its wilder excesses by Vancouver Island, a large landmass offshore. Fjords, wooded hills and bays, and a fringe of high mountains form a backdrop. Coming in to land, I'm surprised how extensive the city is. Houses sprawl across the valley from the mountains on the skyline, and disappear out of sight below the wings of the plane. In the centre, where the harbour sits on a deep inlet, an island of skyscrapers, like Manhattan, glints and flashes in the mid-day sun.

Immigration and customs are incredibly easy, for someone used to the stringent controls and the endless queues at British airports. There's a casual, happy atmosphere. I feel immediately more relaxed than I did when I set out. And Haida art is there to greet me. The centrepiece of the international terminal is a gigantic bronze sculpture, eighteen feet long and twelve feet high, patinated in green, called The Spirit of Haida Gwaii by Haida artist Bill Reid. It's sometimes called the Jade Canoe because of the subject matter and colour. This sculpture is a copy of the original, patinated in black to resemble argillite, which stands outside the Canadian Embassy in Washington DC.

The big bronze canoe holds a cargo of myth. Sitting at the back is Raven acting as the steersman. Raven is one of the most powerful figures in First Nation mythology, featuring in many of the creation myths. It's interesting that on the other side of the Atlantic, at the same latitude, the Celts and the Vikings also have stories about ravens.

Bill Reid - The Jade Canoe

The Haida people have only two main clans — the Raven and the Eagle. In the legends all the Haida people are descended from two supernatural women. The Raven people come from *Sgulu Jaad* — Foam Woman — and the Eagle people from *Ts'iila Quons* — Volcano Woman. They each had ten children who intermarried. Like many other aboriginal people theirs is a matrilineal society. You take your clan lineage from your mother, so if she is from the Eagle moiety, you will be Eagle too. Traditionally, people could only marry someone from the opposite clan — an Eagle had to marry a Raven and vice versa

— which sounds prescriptive but avoids close intermarriage in small social groups. There's an eagle in the Jade Canoe too, near the front, biting the paw of a bear. This bear is from a story about a Haida princess who married a bear and gave birth to two cubs (Bad Bear and Good Bear) before going back to her people. The whole family is at the front of the canoe, paddling vigorously.

Mousewoman, a small but very important figure in a number of myths, is hiding under Raven's tail, and further along is Dogfish Woman. Beaver is there and Wolf and the Frog who was believed to be a link between the underwater world and the land. In the centre sits a dreaming figure in Haida clothing. This is the spirit of Haida Gwaii, holding a Shaman's staff carved with a killer-whale, a sea-grizzly and a raven. And, almost under his sleeve, is a small human being with a cedar-bark cloak and a spruce-root hat, called the Ancient Reluctant Conscript, who may represent the sculptor himself. Bill Reid said that on every boat that had ever sailed, there was always a reluctant conscript doing the work.

There are many interpretations of the Jade Canoe's meaning, but it seems, from his own accounts of the sculpture's creation, that what Bill Reid intended was to represent the natural environment and the interdependence of all creatures on each other. Human beings and animals rely on each other for their mutual survival, even though they aren't always in harmony with each other. In other words, we're all in the same canoe. The fact that Raven, regarded by the Haida as a 'cunning trickster', is holding the steering oar is thought to be symbolic, in the artist's mind, of the unpredictability of the natural world.

Out of the air-conditioned terminal building the heat is almost overwhelming — a record breaking 27 degrees for May. According to the TV screens I'd been watching while I queued through immigration, it is even hotter inland and wild fires have broken out in the forests to the north. I feel dismayed, because I've brought only cool, northern, outdoor clothes and everyone around me is in shorts and bikini tops. I haven't even brought a dress.

My first night is spent in a motel near the airport, which, viewed online, I'd assumed was quite convenient. As a budget

21

traveller I hope to walk as much as possible and use public transport. But I'd underestimated just how big Vancouver is. The motel is quite close to the airport as the crow flies, but a complex journey on dual carriageways and flyovers that can't be negotiated on foot or by public transport. The helpful lady at the airport tells me to take a taxi.

The staff are Chinese and very polite. I've been allocated a smoker's room, which is a problem, and I have to pay an extra C$20 for an upgrade as there aren't any other non-smoking rooms left. I've been in the country less than three hours and already I've spent C$40 more than I'd budgeted for. My room is adequate, but it's obvious that I can't stay there. I can't afford to take a taxi every time I need to go out. Tomorrow morning I will have to move.

Eating is also going to be a problem. This isn't an area where there are restaurants or cafés. After I've unpacked I wander out to explore and discover a small row of shops; a drive-in burger bar (closed), a furniture store, a dentist and a Chinese grocer. There, among the unfamiliar goods and packaging, I find what I hope is a pot noodle kit (the instructions are in Mandarin) that I can fill from the coffee machine in my room, as well as some cereal bars, biscuits and an ice cream. Exhausted by the unexpected heat, my inappropriate clothes, and the time difference, I sit on a wall beside the road and eat the ice cream before it drips down my arm.

It's the middle of the night UK time and I feel thoroughly travel-lagged. The landscape in front of me is visually strange and totally un-European. Big bull-nosed American semis surge past, with loud klaxons and exhaust stacks belching diesel fumes. The road in front of me is a six lane highway, but with lots of trees and electricity lines knotted on poles along the side of the road. The houses remind me of New Zealand — chalet type bungalows with wooden facades and decking; big ranch-style modern houses and the occasional art-deco gem, all fence-to-fence beside each other. I have one of those 'What am I doing here?' moments. So far from home, spending so much money, eating junk food in the wrong clothes, in the wrong motel. You must be mad, I tell myself, and feel very small and vulnerable and homesick.

Jet lag is a strange thing. You lose the ability to calculate time — I don't know whether five minutes have elapsed or fifty. There's an odd feeling of physical disorientation and loss of spatial awareness — putting something down and then not being able to remember what you did with it. Everything has to be done with exaggerated care. And then there's the narcolepsy. One moment you're eating a nice meal in a nice restaurant (or a pot noodle in your room) and the next you're unconscious face down in your plate. Nothing does any good but rest and time.

Next morning I relocate to a new motel in a different part of the city. The area is almost completely Chinese. I had noticed when I left the airport that all the signage was in English, French and Mandarin, but I hadn't expected to find such a large Chinese population here. I'm told that Vancouver is a Rainbow City, with one of the most varied ethnic mixes of any major urban centre. 52% of the population have a first language other than English. As well as French, European, American, Japanese, Inuit and Pacific Islander, it has a big Asian population; there are areas where you can live and work and never have to speak any language other than Mandarin. My second motel is also Chinese-run, clean and bright, with wide comfortable mattresses and fluffy pillows. I have the choice of two king-size beds in my tiny room. It also serves breakfast, which is very useful. The buses that run past the door are frequent, clean and fast and have bicycle racks on the front. They connect with the Sky Train service so I can travel anywhere in the city to visit all the places I have on my list.

The most important of these is the Museum of Anthropology on the campus of the University of British Columbia which, I soon discover, is one of the biggest universities in North America. It's as large as a small town, with schools and shopping malls and its own bus service. There are more than 34,000 students, not counting the academic and ancillary staff. It occupies a magnificent position on a piece of land curving out into the ocean with gorgeous views of mountains and sea.

This land belongs to the Musqueam First Nation. Their name

means 'People of the Grass' and refers to their traditional lands, on the foreshore around the mouth of the Fraser River, where eelgrass grew in abundance. They are one of the richest 'Bands' in Canada, which is hardly surprising since such a prosperous city has been built on what were once their villages and ancestral burial places. A 'Band' is a unit of government among First Nation people, established by the Indian Act of 1876. Bands aren't allowed to actually own land 'reserved' for them, the legal title to the reserve is vested in the Crown who holds it in trust for the Band, who can run their own businesses there, or lease sections to others. Usually they were allotted the least profitable land. As Chief Clarence Louie of the Osoyoos Band in the Okanagan put it recently, 'They gave the best land to the European newcomers and stuck the Indians back in the bush and gave them bread and water and a Bible.'[3] But some Bands were luckier and the Musqueam was one of them.

It is a Musqueam artwork that welcomes you to the Museum. Susan Point's stone floor, Salish Pathway, is a swirling mosaic of coloured stone that suggests birds and fish and animals in abstract patterns. The artist explains that, 'the imagery is based on the whorls and lines of a thumb or toe print, transformed using distinctive Salish elements, and incorporating many of the life forms found in the land, sea, and skies surrounding the Museum of Anthropology. [It] emphasizes the Salish connection to the site — a reminder that the surrounding land is Musqueam traditional territory and a welcome from the Musqueam people to this territory.'[4]

Once inside, you're in an airy cathedral of light. It was created by one of Canada's leading architects, Arthur Erickson. Part of his brief was to create a space that would take some of the biggest totems and the result is breathtaking. The Musqueam Band are part of a broader group known as the 'Coast Salish', who built their wooden houses in a very particular way with two carved upright poles at the front, supporting a carved cross beam. The architecture of the museum has taken this idea with a series of concrete upright and cross beams filled in with walls of glass.

Inside, the totems stand erect in all their complexity and

Museum of Anthropology, Vancouver

beauty. I have only seen them in photographs and I'm not prepared for their size, or their emotional impact. I hadn't realised how tall they are, or how wide, carved from gigantic old-growth trees. They were created to make a statement about lineage, to record the histories of the clan, and to impress visitors with their power. The painter Emily Carr, who saw them in their original locations in the abandoned villages, said that they were the product of 'strong thought'. I am unexpectedly moved. There's a skip in the heartbeat, an involuntary intake of breath when you stand in front of them.

The Haida poles are immediately recognisable. The carving is unique. Haida art has definite, flowing lines, particularly around the eyes and the carving is very deep. Each form is connected to the others in a complex and visually satisfying way; creatures emerge from other creatures' mouths and ears, they perform transformations, peer between the legs of supernatural beings, are carried on the backs of killer whales, each merging seamlessly into the other. Everything, as the Haida say, is connected.

On the carved cedar chests the painted forms follow the same patterns, but on a flat surface, the animals, fish and birds are

25

A Haida housepole from the Museum of Anthropology

flattened out and taken to a high level of abstraction. Haida artists call these 'formlines' and a creature can be unravelled and splayed out in Picasso-like fashion, but is still recognisable. Some of these lines resemble the intricate whorls of a fingerprint. This art is extremely sophisticated and curiously modern.

It's here, in the Museum, that I get the first chance to learn more about the mysterious figure known as D'Sonoqua (sometimes spelled Dzunukwa). She was the black, red-lipped Wild Woman of the Forest, but also Mother Earth; fierce, fertile, nurturing, both the bringer and the taker of life, to be feared and respected. You angered her at your peril. Children were particularly afraid of her, because she sometimes stole bad children and ate them. When I first read about D'Sonoqua, I was reminded of the Goddess Kali, who is also black, red-lipped and the bringer of both good and evil. Kali is a mother goddess, created first, before light came to the world, which explains why she is black, but she is also a violent and destructive force — the wife of 'the Lord of Death'. D'Sonoqua, like Kali, is more than a figure to frighten naughty children with, linking back to something more primitive and powerful.

Here in the Museum are some D'Sonoqua masks once used in ritual dances. They are painted black with hollow, unseeing eyes and open mouths. You can still see the attachments where animal hair was placed around the head. The masks I already knew about, and had seen pictures of in books on First Nation art, but I didn't expect the D'Sonoqua feast dishes. They are made from a big piece of cedar, carved into the life-size form of D'Sonoqua, her belly hollowed out to become a gigantic vessel for food. The significance of eating from a woman's belly is easy to understand, but in a matrilineal society, where women were such an important source of knowledge and power it has another level.

I spend all day in the Museum trying to learn as much as I can about First Nation societies and their history. I eat salmon chowder in the café and walk outside into the garden, where a replica Haida village has been built on the shores of a small lake with totem poles and spectacular views over the city of Vancouver to the mountains beyond. Across the strait you can also see Vancouver Island.

Part of the site for the museum was a circular gun turret that had been built during the Second World War and the architect was asked to incorporate it into the design if possible. A circular gallery was created with a glass roof and Bill Reid was commissioned to produce a carving to fit the space. The result is 'Raven and the First Men'. It's part of the Haida creation myth carved from a single (gigantic) piece of yellow cedar. Raven sits on top of a clam shell as human beings struggle inside, and the plaque beside the carving tells the story in Bill Reid's own words.

'*The great flood, which had covered the earth for so long, had at last receded and the sand of Rose Spit, Haida Gwaii, lay dry. Raven walked along the sand, eyes and ears alert for any unusual sight or sound to break the monotony. A flash of white caught his eye and there, right at his feet, half buried in the sand, was a gigantic clam shell. He looked more closely and saw that the shell was full of little creatures cowering in terror in his enormous shadow. He leaned his great head close and, with his smooth, trickster's tongue, coaxed and cajoled and coerced them to come out and play in his wonderful shiny new world. These little dwellers were the original Haidas, the first humans.*'

Bill Reid - Raven and the First Men

A museum is not the best place to see these things in. The First Nation artefacts are out of context and that robs them of some of their meaning. Children are running around shrieking, tourists walk in front of you with large cameras, there are loud American accents and chattering Chinese. An English couple behind me have just asked, in strident voices, if they can get in free because they haven't much time. "We've only got twenty minutes!" I hear the woman say. But in spite of the background noise, I've learned a lot and seen things I couldn't possibly have seen anywhere else.

Outside, sitting by the lake before I leave to find a bus back into the city, I try to think it all through. Are these mythologies I'm learning about any use to us in present day society? Or are they simply lovely stories from the past, told by people struggling to understand the world around them, just as we are now? Are they only valuable to the people whose legacy they are, or can Europeans learn from them too? We can no longer get into the mind-set of the people who created them, who had a different relationship to the landscape and a different world view. Our minds and our genes have been altered by our culture. We see with the eyes of our time, interpret everything with a 21st century, globally influenced, understanding. We can't un-know centuries of scientific knowledge; we can never truly leave behind our Western, capitalist educations. Is it possible to learn something from their stories, perhaps enough to create a new story for ourselves, a new mythology to teach us how to live in the messed up world we find ourselves in? We treated these people like animals and we trashed their culture as obsolete, but perhaps it's time to admit that we were wrong and they were right.

These are some of the questions I've come here to answer.

3. Art or Anthropology

*'The joy of the wild is rooted deep in the human spirit and
without it our lives are starved of a vital nutrient.'*
Grant A. Mincy, *The Ecologist*, 23rd May 2015

I take the Skytrain down to the waterfront in the heart of Vancouver, except that the Skytrain from here is completely underground. It's also eerily unmanned. There are automatic ticket
machines, automatic entry gates, escalators, video surveillance,
disembodied voices making announcements, and driverless
trains that slide into the station and silently disappear again.
It's the epitome of a modern technological city.

I emerge into the old station terminus, which is an elegant
colonial building that has a certain presence. The long facade is
unusual, built from red brick with classical white columns, and
it's typical of nineteenth century 'power dressing'. It's the kind of
building that makes you think about how the English peasants
in their single-storey huts might have reacted to the gigantic
monuments of stone that the Normans raised in almost every
town in England, to subdue the spirits of the natives and remind
them of the hopelessness of resistance. The station terminal feels
very much like that.

I'm not a fan of cities; they've come to represent everything
that is problematic about the way we live. They are cathedrals
of capitalist culture, making visible the mantra of endless
growth and consumption. These days, I find them frightening
— one day without power, water or sanitation and they would be
uninhabitable, and the millions who live here rendered hysterical
with fear.

I lived through the Christchurch earthquake and remember the terror of turning on a tap and nothing coming out, with two small children in the house who couldn't do without drinking water for long. The sewage system had also been damaged and we had to dig a latrine at the bottom of the garden. The lack of power was easier to cope with, but the bank tills didn't work and supermarkets (those that were undamaged) couldn't sell anything because the tills that controlled the stock inventories were down. Petrol stations weren't functioning either. No money equals no fuel, no food, no water. Cities are perilous places.

Downtown Vancouver

Central Vancouver has long straight streets laid out on gridlines with high rise buildings on every side. This is 'Downtown', which is Canadian for the City Centre. I'd imagined a waterfront where I could sit with a coffee or a glass of wine and look out to sea, but it's all cruise liners and container ships. There probably are such places, but you probably have to know where to go and how to get there. I feel a sense of frustration. The distances are daunting on foot. I'm a good walker, but it takes me twenty minutes to cover what looks, on the map, like a couple of blocks. To cheer myself up I have a coffee and Belgian chocolate waffles in a café under an office block in a concrete canyon.

I locate the Bill Reid Gallery in a beautiful art deco house dwarfed on either side by high-rise blocks and a shopping mall. There's an incongruous flashing sign outside for the parking lot underneath. But the gallery itself is fascinating. Bill Reid was one of Canada's foremost artists. He was born in 1920 to a Scottish German father and a Haida mother who came from the village of T'aanu on Haida Gwaii. She was a member of the Raven/Wolf clan. Bill had a fairly conventional upbringing and became a radio announcer for the Canadian Broadcasting Company's radio station in Toronto. He had always had an aptitude for art and had begun carving objects out of blackboard chalk when he was still at school. In the gallery there's a minute, delicate tea service he carved when he was twelve, each item smaller than my little finger nail, decorated with his sister's nail polish. The tiny teapot even has a detachable lid. He also carved totem poles out of columns of chalk.

While working for CBC he began to do more research into Haida art. Bill's life changed when he visited Haida Gwaii in 1954 and saw work by Charles Edenshaw, the great Haida sculptor who had once taught Bill's maternal grandfather. After that visit, he said, "the world was not the same." Bill studied gold and silver-smithing and started creating jewellery — one of the areas in which Charles Edenshaw excelled — and made some stunning pieces, now collector's items, combining both Haida and European ideas. But as Bill came to understand the symbolism and mythological references better, he began to carve in wood. He studied the original forms and techniques and tried to bring traditional art into the twentieth century. Bill was also instrumental in rescuing some of the most important totems from the abandoned villages for preservation in the Museum of Anthropology and, in the 1980s, he was actively involved in the anti-logging protests that saved the rainforests of the southern island of Moresby and the Gwaii Haanas National Park. He was multi-talented and had a parallel career as a poet, broadcaster and author. He died in 1998.

Bill's funeral chest is in the gallery, carved and painted by a friend. His body was taken by canoe, a two day journey from Victoria to T'aanu, the village on Moresby Island — now abandoned — where his mother had been born. His emblems are on the chest; the Raven, because that was his moiety, and the Wolf, because that was his clan. The canoe, Lootaas, which means 'Wave-eater', was a fifteen metre war canoe that Bill himself had carved for Expo 86 out of a single piece of cedar.

The Bill Reid Gallery, Vancouver

There are examples in the gallery of almost every type of work by the artist. 'Mythic Messengers' is a large bronze wall plaque, braiding figures from mythology together, connecting them with their long tongues. It's subtitled 'Sharing tongues, Bridging the Gap between Communities'. There are masks, robes and other ceremonial regalia, jewellery and traditional Haida argillite carvings as well as paintings and contemporary sculptures. The images have a power that can still be felt.

Other First Nation artists, many of them mentored by Bill Reid, are also exhibited there. Some of them are descendants of Charles Edenshaw; established names like James Hart, Robert Davidson, Guujaaw, as well as members of a younger generation like Ernest Swanson, Tyson Brown, Jaalen and Gwaai Edenshaw. The young sculptors are examples of how the traditional arts are being handed on in British Columbia, in an attempt to preserve the old knowledge before it dies out. An eight foot pole by Gwaai Edenshaw, carved in yellow cedar and cast in bronze, was being exhibited. It represents a supernatural being called *Godanxee'wat*, or Stone Ribs, who is one of the Haida ancestors.

Gwaai Edenshaw is connected with the Haida Gwaii Rediscovery Youth Program, which awards the name Stone Ribs to young people who have successfully completed one of Rediscovery's two-week immersion courses. The Program transports young people to remote, traditional locations where they leave the modern world behind and live as their ancestors did. They learn how to survive and live off the land without electricity or any of the conveniences of twenty-first century life. It is designed to re-connect them to their own history and their relationship with the land and sea.

Among the Haida it seems that art and politics go together. Gwaai's father, Guujaaw, was a famous political activist during the time that members of the Haida Nation were trying to get their land back and applying for World Heritage Status for some of the abandoned villages on Moresby Island, and the protected area known as Gwaii Haanas. Bill Reid was also able to use his status as writer and artist to help the Haida cause. He stopped work on his sculpture 'The Spirit of Haida Gwaii', commissioned to sit outside the Canadian Embassy in Washington DC, as a protest during the tussle over logging in the 1980s. The tradition of protest goes on. In the gallery I watch a video made by the young singer and artist Kinnie Starr, in support of the 'Save Our Whales' campaign.

Just up the street from the Bill Reid Gallery, the Vancouver City Art Gallery is an imposing, classically inspired, colonial building with a portico and Greek columns. As I walk up to it I can see that there is a huge demonstration happening outside on the steps and in the small garden at the front. There are people holding placards, buskers playing music and there are stalls selling a variety of crafts and food. Families are picnicking on the grass with children. A man holding a microphone is standing on the steps talking about GM foods and Monsanto spraying. A parked pick-up, which has seen a few miles pass under the wheels, has a number plate that reads NON-GMO. It's loaded with organic plants. The demonstration is friendly and passionate and very well organised, but just around the corner there's a posse of police on motor cycles — presumably just in case. They don't seem happy to be photographed, so I put my camera away.

Demo at Vancouver Art Gallery

Vancouver Art Gallery is a great disappointment. The gallery is being totally re-furbished — builders everywhere and blank, empty galleries where I'd expected the permanent collection to be. There's a notice in one room that mentions Cezanne, though the walls are bare; in another a photograph of Jacques Lipschitz is on the wall. Lipschitz came from Lithuania to settle in America at the beginning of the Second World War. In 1963 he was persuaded by an Italian artist called Fiore de Henriquez, who lived in a complicated triangle with him and his wife for a time, to come to Pietrasanta in Italy. Through my partner, who is a sculptor in Pietrasanta, we came to know Fiore well and through her, the work of Lipschitz. Finding his photograph on the wall makes an eerie connection between my life in Italy and my presence in Vancouver, but is also an example of the pervasive influence of European art across the globe.

I've come because I know that the City Art Gallery has an extensive collection of paintings and drawings by early twentieth century Canadian artist Emily Carr and, because they staged a big exhibition of the work of Charles Edenshaw the previous year, I'd anticipated that they would have a representative selection of indigenous art. When I go to a city art gallery I expect to get some sense of its artistic history and tradition, as well as a glimpse of what's going on now. On the top floor, in one small room, there are a few of Emily Carr's tree paintings and drawings supposedly 'in dialogue' with a video installation by a group of contemporary artists. It's very disappointing. Apart from the fact that occasionally there is something that resembles a shimmering landscape and occasionally some of the frames are green, I can't see any kind of relationship at all. The banging of builders removes any kind of atmosphere.

Thoroughly disgruntled, I find my way to the café, which has an outside garden and some very nice local Sauvignon Blanc wine. The pear, fennel and parsnip soup turns out to be surprisingly tasty, with a watercress and grapefruit salad. It's a great improvement on pot noodles.

Revived by this indulgent and very late lunch, I go back into the gallery. On the lower floor, there's a sparse and rather forlorn exhibition of young contemporary artists but it feels unbelievably weak and Euro-centric after seeing what is being produced by the young artists still working in First Nation traditions. The exhibition is called 'The Poetics of Space' and there isn't a single painting or installation that shows the slightest hint that the artist has understood what it means. A young guide is trying to explain it to a group of visitors and failing miserably.

European art has become unanchored. Tradition has long since been abandoned. Without roots, or a strong tradition to draw on, it sways in the wind of fashion. I look at the progeny of my own culture in this gallery and think, 'What are they doing here?' and I realise suddenly that there's not a single indigenous work of art anywhere on display. That makes me very, very angry. Why are the descendents of European colonial culture being exhibited here and the descendents of indigenous residents being exhibited in the museum of anthropology? It makes no sense. And why is the work of Bill Reid — one of the greatest artists that British Columbia has ever produced — in the Museum of Anthropology and not here? James Hart, Charles Edenshaw, Gwaai Edenshaw, Robert Davidson? Where are they?

It makes me suspect that there is Art Apartheid being practised here, because it is a shameful fact that in many countries, the artwork of indigenous people is almost always 'anthropology' rather than fine art, despite the fact that their art comes from one of the most ancient traditions in the world. In the words of a British Museum curator; 'Aboriginal art represents one of the longest unbroken art traditions in the world, going back at least 40,000 years.' Too often, cultural apartheid is being practised. Even when we have re-instated First Nation people's democratic rights of citizenship, their culture has been left behind. New Zealand is one example of a country that has worked very hard to preserve its aboriginal heritage. Children in primary school learn the Maori language and the values of its culture. They learn its mythologies. But it's not just the First Nation people who are not represented here — Vancouver has a big Chinese population whose work is also absent from the walls.

The prestigious architects Herzog and de Meuron are designing a new Vancouver Art Gallery, which will, according to the blurb, have a commitment 'to the diverse communities we live in'. The projected date for opening is 2021 in its new location. It will connect 'the past' (images shown are of a group of white European men dated around 1910), the present (a photograph of another group of white European men) and the future (left blank). Indigenous art and the huge ethnic (and gender) diversity of British Columbia has a long time to wait.

I glance at the newspaper on the bus back to the motel and the front page article is about the price of property in Vancouver which, parents fear, will make it impossible for their children, the new 'Millenials', to continue to live in the city. By a strange coincidence, the Poem in Transit today is 'Fever' by Jennica Harper, also about the problems of affordable housing in Vancouver. It features a hopeful young woman browsing the online property sites and finding that she would even have to pay 'Three quarters of a mil/ for a tear down.' Property prices here are as high as London.

On impulse, I get off the bus at the Pacific Central Station to investigate transport to Victoria. I hadn't intended to go across to Vancouver Island so soon, but I'm not enjoying this city and, without local knowledge, I'm not going to find the small, out of the way, places I need to find for another perspective. Cities are big, lonely places. Victoria might not be any better, but I can at least find out more about Emily Carr and then do a bit of exploring on Vancouver island before heading north to Haida Gwaii.

At the station, where the Amtrak trains arrive from America, I discover that I can get a coach that will take me directly from Vancouver to Victoria city centre, including the ferry transit. It's reassuringly cheap. I take a deep breath and book it. If I don't like Victoria I can always get a bus or a ferry somewhere else.

On the television in my room that evening, I hear the phrase, 'Truth and Reconciliation'. I don't know what it means, but everyone here is talking about it.

4. Emily Carr

'Life is like a whole packet of firecrackers going off at once without even waiting for the match'.
EC Letter to Edythe Hembroff, Nov. 1936

If indigenous art has had an uphill struggle to find a place in a euro-centric culture, Emily Carr, as a gifted nineteenth century woman, experienced a similar process of discouragement and disapproval because of her gender. Described as a 'genius' by the art critic of the *Manchester Guardian* in 1938 after an exhibition of Canadian art at the Tate Gallery, she is now regarded as one of Canada's leading authors and artists, but it wasn't always that way.

Emily was born in Victoria in 1871, the same year that British Columbia became part of the Canadian Federation. She was the youngest of five daughters and her life followed the pattern of most precocious girls at the end of the 19th century. She could draw from an early age and her father, for whom she was something of a favourite, paid for her to have lessons — the kind that were given to refined ladies. Her family life was otherwise quite narrow, within the deeply respectable confines of colonial society in Victoria, a city that Emily likened to 'a lying-down cow, chewing'. Emily's mother and father came originally from Kent and it seemed to Emily that their aim, like most expatriates, was to re-create England in Canada. Her father, she wrote, 'had buried a tremendous homesickness in his new soil and it had rooted and sprung up English'.

Her birth wasn't recorded in the family Bible until that of her small brother, born two years later. Of this event, Emily wrote

Emily Carr with one of her beloved dogs.

in her memoir *Growing Pains*: 'The covers of the Bible banged, shutting us all in'. Religion, a conservative Protestanism, created the bars of the cage that held them. Her sisters, she wrote, found the human body so sinful that they could only take a bath in a darkened room, wearing a bathing costume. Emily was similarly inhibited when she was young and only one of the sisters ever married. Their brother died before reaching adulthood.

By the time that Emily's baby brother was born, her mother was already sick. Mrs Carr had given birth to more than eight children — two other boys had died in infancy. She faded away in an upstairs room and was dead by the time Emily was twelve. Mr Carr died two years later, leaving Emily and her siblings in the care of their eldest sister. It was not, Emily remarked wryly, 'a nest of doves'. There was considerable conflict. That, she implied was partly what 'drove her' to the woods, and what powered her art. Emily wanted to carry on her art studies and persuaded her father's trustees to advance the money to pay for her to go to San Francisco to study art. She was very excited and hoped that this was an opportunity to escape from her family and begin a career in art. But after only a year, her hopes foundered on the family's diminishing finances and her sisters' disapproval.

Emily was drawn to the indigenous 'Indian' population as a young girl. 'Just across the harbour was the Songhees Indian reserve. I loved anything to do with Indians. The reserve was a glory place for adventure to my imagination — it was forbidden absolutely to children, but one could look across at it from father's store.'[5] She was also drawn to the immense, impenetrable forests of British Columbia. Susan Vreeland's novel about Emily Carr's life is called *The Forest Lover*, a reference to the way she painted it obsessively. Emily often asked herself, in her diaries, what it was about the forest that drew her in. 'What is that vital thing the woods contain, possess, that you want? Why do you go back and back to the woods unsatisfied, longing to express something that is there and not able to find it?'[6]

She began to go on painting trips to the remoter parts of Vancouver island 'prospecting for art', to places like Ucluelet and Alert Bay, where she painted the people and the carved poles that were, to her, very strange and the subject of wonder. The landscape was overwhelming. 'No boundaries no beginnings no ends … No artist I knew, no art school had taught art this size.' Received opinion was that Western Canada was boring and unpaintable. Emily began by 'nibbling at the edges', sketches and watercolours of the houses and the people. Later she found a Haida man and his wife who had a 'good boat' and they took her to Haida Gwaii where she painted the abandoned villages and the poles that had been left to rot where they stood on the shoreline. Emily intended it to be the record of a vanishing culture and hoped that the government would buy her paintings, but she was too far ahead of her time. Discouraged and humiliated by the public response, financially affected by a global recession, Emily gave up painting for fifteen years.

Emily Carr is the main reason that I've come to Victoria but, on the walk from the bus station to my motel through the city centre, I've already decided that I like this place. It is mostly low-rise, with a lot of old buildings and views of the harbour. There are quirky bars and shops and a great deal of character. I can see why the city ranks so high in the list of 'best places to live'. After a grey, cloudy ferry trip I was soon sitting beside the thermally heated swimming pool which, unexpectedly, my motel had, sipping a cold glass of local white wine and feeling good, looking up at a blue sky. The heatwave persists here. Fog comes in off the ocean overnight and through the morning, but burns off by lunchtime.

I met an interesting couple on the bus. Cy is a writer from LA, travelling with his wife Wanda, and has written for every comedy series on US TV from Bob Newhart to Frasier (including Rhoda and House). They were both fascinating — she had been in Bolivia with the Peace Corps and was very politically engaged with South America; he was full of anecdotes and self-mockery. 'You think what you're doing's wonderful at the time,' he said. 'But later on you realise that it was crap!' It's a pity I won't see them again. Oddly, Cy was more timid than his wife and confessed that he didn't enjoy travelling much. But Wanda loved it. She was always darting off to check something out, while he worried about missing connections, double checking tickets. We parted promising to meet for a drink, but I think it unlikely, as he is staying at the best hotel in Victoria and I am in budget accommodation on the other side of town.

The motel is very comfortable and the breakfasts here are staggering. I'm eating a bowl of porridge big enough to concrete a patio, and the guy on the table next to me has a heaped plate of eggs, hash browns and assorted dead animal parts that defies imagination. There's a strong, saliva inducing smell of bacon. My resolution to be healthy and eat less meat is being challenged here!

I listen to some guys talking in the café during breakfast, and they are discussing fishing and flying float-planes, telling each other anecdotes such as "He forgot to put the landing gear down, but they still paid out on the insurance", and recommending that, "You take your wallet out of your pocket before you lower your gear" when salmon fishing. Apparently if you don't, you can find your wallet at the bottom of the ocean.

Emily Carr's Family House.

Afterwards I walk downtown to find Emily Carr's family house, which is preserved as a museum. It's a pretty, double-fronted wooden house in colonial style, painted yellow. You can sit in the conservatory and read Emily's books, or wander round the garden before exploring the interior. The breakfast room, dining room and two small parlours are furnished in nineteenth century style as accurately as possible, though not everything belonged to the Carrs. Emily's typewriter sits on a small table and her paintings decorate the walls. It has a peaceful feel — sitting among the trappings of the successful Victorian middle class; the antique tables with lace cloths and fragile bone china, gilt-framed mirrors and velvet covered sofas. They even shipped out their pianos from England on sailing ships travelling for thousands of miles of turbulent ocean, all the way down the Atlantic, round the hazardous Cape Horn and then up the Pacific coast. After the railways were built, goods could be offloaded in Hudson Bay and then freighted across Canada by train, but it still cost a lot. A piano in the parlour was a big status symbol.

The Carrs were typical of the affluent middle classes. Mr Carr had a dry-goods store in the centre of Victoria and his house stood on ten acres of land hacked from the forest on what was then the outskirts of town. The street was originally called Carr Street, but it became Government Street, to acknowledge the Parliament building that was erected shortly after Emily was born. Both street names are displayed. After his death, the girls gradually sold off plots of land in order to support themselves and the house is now surrounded by other, similar structures. Emily herself built an apartment block round the corner, containing four flats, to provide an income. She called it the 'House of All Sorts' and hoped to support herself in order to have time to paint. But the First World War arrived with all its financial difficulties and soon earning a living took up all her time. Her eccentric mix of tenants gave her endless excuses for complaint and procrastination.

Emily was jolted out of her retirement in 1927, aged 56, when she received a call from the National Gallery of Canada, requesting some paintings for an exhibition. Suddenly, her work was in demand, but she felt that it had come too late. 'How little I've accomplished!' she wrote. 'And the precious years are flying by and never, never one minute will the clock tick backwards.'[7]

Emily acquired a rather primitive caravan, which she would have towed to a roadside location in the forest and she would camp there during the summer, painting and enjoying some solitude, accompanied by several dogs, her pet monkey and a rat. There's a beautiful entry in her diary that records how she went bathing in the river on a moonlit night, slipping into the cool water, becoming one with the elements. When Emily's heart began to give trouble, she started to write books — short stories and memoirs. She said that 'trying to find the equivalents for things in words' helped her 'to find the equivalents in painting.' Her prose is lyrical and completely original. It wasn't surprising that the autobiographical *Klee Wyck* won awards when it was published in 1941. The nursing home where she spent her last weeks is just around the corner from the Carr house, and is now a hotel called the James Bay Inn. Emily died from heart failure in 1945.

Emily Carr's family parlour with piano

I walk down Government Street back to the city centre, with my head firmly in Emily Carr's life and her struggle to realise her potential against so much family and public opposition. I pass the sprawling, gothic Parliament building fronting onto the harbour and see that here, too, there's a demonstration. This time it's against pollution. The people of Canada are not standing quietly by while corporate factions ruin their land and their livelihoods.

In the harbour the Coho ferry is manoeuvring out of its berth on its way to Seattle. My American acquaintances are probably on it, heading back to California. A couple of float-planes are skittering across the water to offload more 'Whale Watch' customers. Sightings guaranteed, pledges the sign. Wild-life tourism is very big business here.

Overlooking the harbour, in front of the nineteenth century gothic Empress Hotel, there's a statue of Captain Cook, whose fault this all is. Captain James Cook RN arrived on the coast of Vancouver Island in 1778, March 31st, in his ship Discovery. He'd been looking for the Pacific exit of the fabled North West Passage and moored for repairs in a bay he named Friendly Cove. He thought that the local name for it was Nootka — not realising that the natives shouting Nootka, Nootka! were actually telling Cook to bring his ship round into a calmer mooring.

Emily Carr's typewriter

The natives, Cook recorded, were exceptionally friendly and welcoming. They came out in their canoes, with the person Cook believed to be the Chief standing up in the main canoe wearing a painted mask and a hide cloak. According to the record, this figure jumped up and down, raising his head and waving his hands, doing a kind of welcome dance while the others in the canoe made a percussion with their paddle handles on the wooden sides. A reconstruction of this ceremony was filmed by an early photographer, Edward S. Curtis, and included in a supposed documentary *In the Land of the Head Hunters*, which was in fact a silent film, a western inspired fictional representation of life among the indigenous peoples. It has some interesting aspects, but has to be watched with this in mind.

The people who went out to greet Cook and his ships were wealthy and powerful and already had a strong system of government and a vibrant trading economy. They were confident and secure in a culture that had been developing for thousands of years. If they had known that Cook's arrival presaged dispossession, death and destruction, they would have either fled in terror or been more aggressive in repulsing him. Cook's 'discovery', as in other parts of the world, meant the end of their way of life and heralded what has come to be described as 'cultural genocide'.

Captain Cook's ships in the bay at Nootka.

Cook actually died in Hawaii shortly afterwards, but one of his officers, Midshipman George Vancouver, returned to appropriate the land for the British Crown the following year. And after him came waves of traders, keen to buy the sea otter skins the natives had offered them, which the British traded in China. It was a very lucrative market and there was a big demand. Only when the sea otter was almost extinct did the indigenous population call a halt to allow the animals to breed. After the traders came the settlers and immediately there was a clash of cultures. Under the British Columbia Act 1858, ancestral lands were appropriated and indigenous people could be forcibly removed to 'Reserves'. It didn't matter that there were three native people to every European immigrant. They had no say in what happened to either their country or themselves. 'It is as if we are absent,' one native Elder wrote. The British referred to them as 'red vagrants' and brushed them aside with contempt.

The attitude of the European immigrants was one of arrogance, noted by the First Nation people first with amazement, then with sadness and finally with a resignation that sprang from hopelessness. 'They come with an unquestioned assumption of confidence,' an Elder wrote. 'They come with a mission to extinguish our beliefs and traditions. They ban our great gatherings; the Potlatch. We are not to display our hereditary possessions. We are not to dance… they have the right to do whatever they want.'[8]

Cultural Imperialism was based on 'widely accepted notions' of subject or inferior races, which helped to 'fuel the imperial acquisition of territories … throughout the nineteenth century'.[9] This is where colonialism has its roots. Jules Harmand wrote in 1910 that, 'It is necessary … to accept as a principle and point of departure the fact that there is a hierarchy of races and civilisations, and that we belong to the superior race and civilisation … the basic legitimation of conquest over native people is the conviction of our superiority, not merely our mechanical, economic and military superiority, but our moral superiority … it underlies our right to direct the rest of humanity.'[10]

This unquestioned belief in entitlement, is reflected in the European literature of the period. There was an arrogance, an assumption of superiority and god-given right at the very centre of colonial culture. Dickens nails it perfectly in his novel *Dombey and Son* written in 1848, around the time that British Columbia was being colonised; 'The earth was made for Dombey and Son to trade in and the sun and moon to give them light. Rivers and seas were formed to float their ships; rainbows gave them promise of fair weather; winds blew for or against their enterprises; stars and planets circled in their orbits, to preserve inviolate a system of which they were the centre.' [11]

Statue of Captain Cook, Victoria.

On the other side of Cook's statue is a plaque erected in 1962 which celebrates the 'Parade of Ships' named on the harbour wall. A series of plaques, erected by descendants of the original settlers, commemorates the ships they arrived in and the triumphalist language pays 'tribute to the pioneers they brought to this new land. The men and women who fought the good fight and built Victoria and British Columbia'. It was not a good fight. We took away the indigenous people's land, their language and their children and I'm beginning to realise just how terrible that was and wonder that I'm welcome here at all.

The plaques on the harbour wall record how colonial occupation was accomplished. A Spanish explorer, Juan Francesco de la Bodega Y Quadra, from Lima, Peru, arguably got there first and Vancouver had tense negotiations with him about their respective claims to the territory. Eventually the British threatened the Americans, Spanish and Russians with military force and they all backed down. The philosopher Edward Said wrote in his study of *Cultural Imperialism* that Britain was 'in an imperial class by itself, bigger, grander, more imposing than any other'. We were the bullies of international politics.

Settlement really got going in the 19th century. A surveyor called James Douglas arrived in the sailing ship Cadboro in 1842. In 1843 Douglas founded Fort Victoria which later expanded from a military and naval base to a civilian town. In the 1840s and 50s whalers and sealers moved in, attracted by the abundant wildlife in the seas off British Columbia. Whales were once so numerous, the white caps of the waves were named for Orca in the indigenous language. You're very lucky to see one now, unless you pay to be taken out on one of the whale sighting expeditions, by plane or boat.

HMS Driver in 1850 brought Richard Blanshard, the first Governor of Vancouver Island. There were about six naval vessels regularly arriving in Victoria harbour to protect British interests, and military personnel kept law and order. Successful merchants became civic figures as British institutions were set up. The first mayor of Victoria was Thomas Harris who came out from Liverpool in 1858, by way of the California goldfields. He made a fortune as a slaughterhouse owner and butcher. On November 16th 1858 the *Panama* sailing out of San Francisco brought Matthew Baillie Begbie as 'Judge of the Crown Colony' of British Columbia. He was later known as 'the hanging judge' because of his uncompromising approach to justice.

Religious institutions quickly followed. The *Marquis of Bute* in 1855 brought Rev and Mrs Edward Cridge to police the colony's Anglican morals. In 1858 the *Seabird* brought four Catholic Sisters of St Anne and less than a year later the *Pacific* brought the first Methodist Missionaries.

Music and Medicine weren't far behind Religion and Justice. *Thames City* brought William Hynes in 1859, bandmaster for the Royal Engineers with his wife. In 1850 the *Norman Morison* brought Dr John Sebastian Helmcken (who married the daughter of James Douglas and was Emily Carr's doctor) and the *Cyclone* brought Dr Nicholles in 1862 with his wife and son. There was no shortage of people willing to take a risk in order to be part of this new venture.

Victoria was also affected by the Canadian Goldrush during the 1850s. Thousands of miners passed through on their way to the gold fields of the Fraser River and the town changed its character and produced hostels, bars, brothels and eateries to cater for them. The *Commodore* was only one of the many ships who brought California Gold Miners on their way to the gold fields of the Fraser River. The gold, iron and copper reserves previously mined by the native people were also plundered by the immigrants.

As I eat my supper in the motel bar I watch the five screens on the walls, my attention flicking from one to the other. There's a range of choices; a brutal Ice Hockey match between the Chicago Blackhawks and the Anaheim Ducks, the French Open tennis tournament, Pacific Hold'em Poker, an interactive Quiz, or the CBC news. The main item on the Canadian news is still Truth and Reconciliation. A report is to be published next week, by a commission set up to investigate the abuses that occurred in the Residential Schools created by the government of British Columbia to forcibly 're-educate' the children of First Nation people and make them into 'proper' Canadians. There are rumblings that the report is going to be very controversial. Cultural Imperialism is being called to account.

5. The Schools of Sorrow

'When a language goes, the voice of the land is silenced'.
Dr Lorna Williams, First People's Cultural Council.

Everyone is so friendly in this small motel, it's like staying with family rather than being in a hotel. I find myself cleaning my room this morning before the maid arrives — making the bed, wiping bath taps and folding towels. It sounds idiotic, but I don't like the idea of someone else cleaning up after me — it makes me feel uneasy. I lived in West Africa for a while when the children were small and, because it was a company house, we had a cook/steward, always referred to locally as a 'boy' however old he was, who scrubbed, cleaned and cooked. His name was Richard and he was highly intelligent, but he'd had very little education. As the middle brother of a large family from a village up-country he had worked, since he was eleven, to send his older brother to school and university. That brother was now a lecturer in history at London University and Richard was working to educate his younger brother as well as supporting his mother and two sisters.

He had been taught to be obsequious towards his employers, calling me Madam all the time (I was twenty three!) and bowing and walking out of rooms backwards in order to respect his Colonial Betters. I couldn't quite come to terms with the fact that this intelligent, clever man was washing my underwear and cleaning my toilet. Richard was my equal. But trying to treat him as one made me enemies among the other Europeans there. I would 'spoil' him; I was giving ideas to other servants (their 'boys'). By paying him more than the pittance that was grudgingly deemed adequate reward for servitude, I was 'ruining the market' for employees (I refused to call him a servant). My experience of the tattered remnants of colonialism, still clinging resolutely to the frangipani trees, left me feeling morally bruised and strengthened my left-wing politics.

One evening we were invited out to dinner at the home of one of the biggest, UK controlled, manufacturing companies in the country. The boss was ex-British public school, and had been living there for thirty years. Dinner was a big formal occasion with silver dishes and several place settings. 'Boys' dressed in white came and went silently, removing plates, serving European food, standing behind our chairs to anticipate anything we might need, such as another drink, the salt cellar, a replacement napkin. Our host had a little bell on the floor under his chair which he pressed with his foot whenever he needed anything. Cigarettes were fetched from a sideboard drawer only a few paces from the table; a book he was telling us about transported from a shelf. It seemed that no personal effort need be expended. One of the guests remarked on how beautifully trained the 'servants' were. To my shock and horror, our host explained how he punished them with a slap when they got it wrong, like naughty children. "They know I won't tolerate sloppy behaviour."

But the final moment of illumination came when I was having a problem with mosquitoes, as it was a very humid evening, and he noticed my discreet attempts to wave them away. He pressed the bell and a 'boy' materialised from the shadows to stand at his shoulder. "Joseph!" our host said in cut-glass tones, "Fetch the Orrff!"

A few moments later Joseph appeared with a can of insecticide on a silver tray. As I stretched out my hand to take it, my host boomed, "Joseph! Spray madam's legs!" And I had to submit to an elderly, dignified man kneeling on the floor in an attitude of subjection to spray my calves with mosquito repellent.

After another gargantuan breakfast (pancakes with maple syrup and a fresh fruit platter), I walk downtown to explore the Museum of British Columbia, which I had passed yesterday on my way to Emily Carr's house. It's a big, modern building with carved totem poles outside and it looks intriguing. Inside I discover an absolute delight. The museum is organised on a timeline of natural and human history and it's all interactive. A full size woolly mammoth greets you with a roar as you enter the natural history section and you wander through the twilit tree trunks of the ancient forest, encountering Elk and other forest creatures, before coming out onto a shoreline with real rock pools, basking seals, sand and seascape. Although the animals are stuffed and it's all a reconstruction, it feels real. You can touch and experience it all at first hand with light and sound. It even smells right.

Mammoth, Victoria Museum

They also have a section on Climate Change. Interestingly, there's no prevarication here, no perhaps, no ifs or buts. Climate Change is accepted as inevitable. British Columbia is warming fast and it's changing the ecology. The displays discuss the plus factors — the crops that can now be grown, plants that you can put in your garden — but also lists the things that are going to be lost. Trees and plants that have long been considered native to Canada will disappear and the animals and insects that depend on them will die out. This process is already being observed by ecologists as pests move north. One of these is the voracious Mountain Pine Beetle which used to be controlled by cold winters where the temperatures sank to minus ten. Warmer winters have allowed it to extend its range and the future looks bleak for its favourite host, the Lodgepole Pine.

There are also warnings about the increasing hazard of wildfires. Summers, the text warns, 'will become hotter, drier and longer'. Climate models apparently show that wildfires will increase 'especially along the coast and in mid-elevation forests of British Columbia'. Some of them are burning now, as I stand in front of the display and, outside the museum, the heatwave shows no signs of abating and there's been no rain since the beginning of May.

It's no accident that one of the world's leading environmentalists, Naomi Klein, comes from British Columbia. She writes that one of her 'wake-up moments' occurred while she was reading a book to her small son, called *Have You Ever Seen a Moose?* She remembered being in Alberta and being told by a member of the Beaver Lake Cree Nation that most of the moose had gone. Those that were left were sick. 'It suddenly hit me: he might never see a moose.'[12] In just over a decade one particular population of moose has dwindled from four thousand to just over a hundred and this has been replicated all over British Columbia. There are lots of theories to account for this, but habitat loss is a significant factor. Moose have vanished completely from areas logged out after being infected by Mountain Pine Beetle. It takes seventy years to restore a de-forested area — far too long for the Moose. The life-like stuffed animals I'm looking at in the museum are also becoming scarce — the wolf, the brown bear and the black bear are not as common as they once were. The sea otter, so nearly extinct, is still a rare sight and only on the largely uninhabited Pacific coast of the islands.

As I move on to the human history section there are some good reconstructions of the archaeology. The first human inhabitants lived in caves and then in pit houses. These were circular, dug down several feet into the earth and then roofed over with a dome of branches, thatched with cedar bark. There was a hole in the middle for smoke to emerge, and it also served as an entrance. A ladder could be pulled up so that predators, like bears, couldn't get in.

Archaeology is currently proving the myths and stories of the First Nation people to be founded in fact. A Haida story about grizzly bears was always thought to be just a story, because there are no grizzlies on Haida Gwaii. But recently the bones of grizzly bears have been found in some locations on the islands, proving that not only was the story true, but that the Haida had been there when a land bridge existed to the mainland some ten thousand years ago. Their stories of the sea rising and then falling also confirm geological events going back almost fourteen thousand years. Mythology can provide a window into the past and is more reliable than we imagine.

As I walk through the timeline I can sit on a bench inside a First Nation house surrounded by artefacts and listen to stories told with the help of wooden masks. There are totem poles and canoes and woven baby baskets, cradle boards for babies, cedar bark clothing, spruce-root hats and a whole range of domestic items; delicate spoons carved from animal horn, shamanic 'sceptres', headdresses for chiefs, carved tobacco pipes, drums made from animal skin, painted chests and argillite platters for feasting. It's all imaginatively laid out to show a way of life. This is one of the best museums I've ever visited.

There's a special exhibition at the moment called 'Living Language'. I stroll into it out of curiosity to hear what the traditional languages sound like, spoken by native speakers. What I find is something much more political and very moving. Colonialism didn't just take away the people's land — it also took away their voices. British Columbia was very rich in indigenous languages; there were about thirty two in the nineteenth century, including three that have no relation to any other language in the world. Haida is one of these 'language isolates'. Linguistic archaeology suggests very diverse origins for the people. There are vocabulary elements in Haida that come from the Pacific Islands, possibly Melanesia. Other elements in First Nation languages suggest

Victoria Museum

migrations from central Asia, or further north in Inuit territory.

The coastal people have a legend about a House of Languages, similar to our own biblical Tower of Babel. The First Ancestors came across a log house full of people, and every person in the house had their own language. These special languages were given as gifts — an acknowledgement of their differences, but the fact that they lived together in one house was a sign of their togetherness in spite of the differences. [13]

The Tutchone people come from Yukon Territory and they have a saying: 'Our Language comes from the Land'. This seems to be common among most indigenous people. There is a strong connection between landscape and language and this explains why, so often, dispossession of land is accompanied by suppression of language. It happened in Britain too, when wealthy English landowners decided to remove inconvenient people from Scottish land they wanted to turn into profitable sheep grazing territory and grouse moor. The Highland Clearances are one of the biggest blots on the English conscience, as whole families, including newborn babies, were turned out of the crofts they had occupied for hundreds of years and left by the roadside to watch their homes and livelihoods burn. Many died of exposure and starvation. The suppression of the Gaelic language was one of the ways in which the English attempted to erase traditional Highland culture and the memory of an entitlement. Land and Language go together, deeply entwined.

One of the things I learned in the exhibition is that there are a lot of false beliefs about aboriginal languages. It isn't true that they are simple, primitive, and unable to handle very complex concepts. They are much more descriptive and poetic than European languages. The five hundred year old body of a man who was found frozen in the melting ice recently is, in the native language, 'Long ago Person Found'. There is even a word for the smell of rain. In another language, thunder is 'Thunderbirds are calling out to one another' — a reference to the mythological beings called Thunderbirds whose wingbeats caused the thunder and whose flashing eyes produced lightning. An entire cultural history is embedded in a language.

It often takes several sentences in English to explain one word, because the words are so specific to the landscape, the culture and the way of life. Australian linguist John Hobson says that aboriginal languages contain 'bodies of knowledge about the environment that simply don't exist in English or the other dominant languages.'[14] For the First Nation people, all their values are enshrined in their language. For instance in Cree, *Put'lt* is a single word that means 'everything belongs to those not yet born'. It expresses the connection language makes to their families, their people and their ancestors. One Cree native speaker says that his language is 'an invisible line from the heart into the past'. This is another reason why languages have to go when you are obliterating a culture, but thousands of years of knowledge and linguistic diversity are lost in the process.

The damage that is done by taking away a language is immense. It is more than simply cutting out someone's tongue and rendering them dumb. You leave people, particularly in an oral culture, without history or roots. You take away their traditions, their links to the landscape, their sense of belonging, their spirituality, their stories and their songs. One Elder said, "Without the language, we are warm bodies without a spirit".[15] But the process of muting a whole community is very difficult to reverse, as a recent evaluation by the University of British Columbia explains.

'[E]ven after the residential school system ended, many adult survivors were too traumatized and ashamed to speak or re-learn their language again. Some others discouraged their children from learning their ancestral language, believing that fluency in English or French would make their lives easier. As a result, generations of Aboriginal peoples are still experiencing the repercussions of language loss.'[16]

In the exhibition, one young mother told of her sadness that she had no nursery rhymes or cradle songs in her traditional language to sing to her new baby. But with the help of her grandmother, she had begun to reconstruct some of the old lullabies and to compose some of her own. As I watch the screen and listen to her singing to her little son, I find myself weeping. No one around me seems to think that this is in any way unusual.

Some of the First Nation Elders are trying to remember (both in the sense of 'recall' and 'put back together') playground songs they had sung as children, before they were taken off to the Residential Schools, so that they can teach them to their grandchildren and great grandchildren. Initially it was very hard to find people who would admit to being native speakers, so great was the sense of shame instilled into them as children. There are very few left now who have an indigenous language as their mother tongue, but there is also a mentoring programme where these Elders (mainly women) work with young people who want to learn their native languages. There is more than language to pass on — all social conventions are enshrined in language, good manners and personal relationships. These young people are re-learning their cultural heritage.

The power of language is underlined by the lengths that the colonial administration was willing to go to, to stamp out the individual tongues. Brutal strategies were adopted by the colonisers to separate the people from their languages, because of their ability to connect and unify communities. There can be no discussion of First Nation languages without talking about the infamous residential schools.

They were set up at the end of the nineteenth century, after amendments to the Indian Act of 1876, with the aim of separating children from their families and culture, in order to 'civilise savages' and assimilate them into the European culture of Canadian society. Children were punished for speaking their own languages, separated from siblings, forbidden to practise their own religion, and — in British Columbia and Alberta — some children were also subjected to sterilisation. In 1907 the death rate of children attending the residential schools was estimated officially at about 40%, yet attendance was made mandatory in 1920 for children between the ages of five and fifteen. The police, and local government officials called 'Indian Agents', forcibly removed children from their homes. Parents who resisted were imprisoned. It is not surprising that they are often referred to as the 'Schools of Sorrow'. The last one in British Columbia only

Children in the Schools of Sorrow

closed in 1986 and the last in Canada a decade later. The Act allowing enforced sterilisation for eugenic reasons, was repealed in 1972.

Within the schools, children in British Columbia, like their Gaelic speaking counterparts in Scotland and Ireland, learned 'English History, English Literature, and an English Imperial world-view'. The education they received was aimed at making them useful workers for their Canadian masters and mistresses. Like the Industrial Schools in Britain, children spent only a small part of the day on academic subjects — most of the time they learned how to be farm labourers, laundry maids, domestic servants and factory workers.[17]

Children in the schools were chronically underfed and this also made them susceptible to disease. Survivors tell how they used to make keys from sardine can openers or spoons and use them to break into the food stores. Some of these crude implements are on display in the museum. The schools were over-crowded, had poor sanitation, lacked heating and there was a distinct absence of medical care — since this had to be paid for. In some schools the death rate was as high as 69%. Survivors reported sadistic corporal punishment. Many are deaf as a result, or have eye and nasal impairments because they were repeatedly hit over the head. Their testimonies make difficult reading.

This history of systemic abuse, like the loss of language, has had life-long repercussions. Recent research has only begun to show how childhood trauma can adversely alter the genetic makeup of an individual and cause disease and ill-health in adults.

'Today … neuroscientists are peering into the once-inscrutable brain-body connection, and breaking down, on a biochemical level, exactly how the stress we experience during childhood and adolescence catches up with us when we are adults, altering our bodies, our cells, and even our DNA.'.[18]

In the exhibition, there are black and white images of children with their teachers inside classrooms or grouped outside on the steps of their schools with nuns and missionaries. None of them look happy. In British Columbia the largest of the schools was St Michael's, on Cormorant Island (where, by coincidence, I'm going next), which could accommodate several hundred children. The photographs show its redbrick four-storey bulk, like a Victorian workhouse, looming above the single-storey wooden houses of the native people. An even greater insult was that it was built on native land — a symbol of oppression and white supremacy.

St. Michael's School, Alert Bay

After the Second World War worse was still to come. The infamous Indian Act was amended in 1951 to allow the forcible removal of children from aboriginal families to be adopted by non-aboriginal families. This social engineering experiment was called the Sixties Scoop, but it continued through the seventies and eighties, causing irreparable harm to individuals, families and communities, who eventually, supported by First Nation lawyers, took collective legal action for compensation for the legacy of the residential schools and the adoption programme.

In 2007 a C\$2 billion compensation package was set up — the largest class action settlement in Canadian history.[19] There were 80,000 eligible claimants. More than 60% of the claims were for ear, nose and throat injuries, but 21% were for orthopaedic conditions caused by broken bones. Claims were also filed for frostbite and limbs lost through industrial accidents in the schools' workshops, laundries and bakeries. One bread-making machine was so dangerous it was known as 'The Mangler'. There is additional compensation for the many victims of sexual abuse who are allowed to give evidence in closed courts.

In response to growing public anger, the Truth and Reconciliation Commission was created in 2008, to try to establish the extent of the abuses and suggest ways of creating a new 'respect for each other and a desire to move forward together with a renewed understanding that strong families, strong communities and vibrant cultures and traditions will contribute to a stronger Canada for all of us'. Prime Minister Stephen Harper made a public apology. He detailed the abuses that the First Nation people had been subjected to and made a full admission of government responsibility.

'The government recognizes that the absence of an apology has been an impediment to healing and reconciliation. Therefore, on behalf of the Government of Canada and all Canadians, I stand before you, in this Chamber so central to our life as a country, to apologize to Aboriginal peoples for Canada's role in the Indian Residential Schools system … There is no place in Canada for the attitudes that inspired the Indian Residential Schools system to ever prevail again… The Government of Canada sincerely apologizes and asks the forgiveness of the Aboriginal peoples of this country for failing them so profoundly.' [20]

I emerge from the museum, blinking into the sun, my eyes prickling with salt, and sit for a while beside the harbour, watching the sun on the water, boats mooring, people going about their lives. Almost everyone is smiling. The contrast with what I've just been reading and hearing is so immense it takes a while to get my balance back. I keep thinking of my own children and my grandchildren, but the emotions that are generated are unbearable. The human capacity for cruelty, it seems, is limitless.

It's my last evening in this lovely city. There's a clear blue sky and the heat radiates from the pavements and the walls of the buildings. Back in the motel for supper, the girl who serves behind the bar is having trouble with her love life. Snatches of conversations and phrases, out of context, drift across my bowl of sticky Thai rice and prawns. The man's voice has a pleading note as he leans across the bar towards her. "Oh, honey, please. Don't do this to me!" She follows him out into the lobby and I can see them entwined in each other's arms for a long and passionate leave-taking. When she comes back there are plenty of customers willing to offer relationship advice as they order their beers. "He's a good guy, you shouldn't let him go." "Trust him and he'll treat you right." "Just `cos you had a bad experience …" And I think of my own man thousands of miles away, in a hot Mediterranean country, who rings me every day whenever the time difference allows, connected to each other across computer servers and satellites, by a tenuous thread of language.

6. Alert Bay

*'For a long time, the wild land was a working place, whether you
were a hunter-gatherer, a crofter, a miner. But now it seems it is
being claimed by the educated middle classes on spiritual quests.'*
Kathleen Jamie, London Review of Books.

Up at 6am. A quick shower, then out into the street with my
luggage. Breakfast is bananas, cashew nuts and biscuits from a
7/11. Before eight o'clock I'm on a Greyhound bus, 'Riding the
Dog' out of Victoria heading north up the east coast of Vancouver
Island to Nanaimo, Campbell River and Port McNeill where I
will get the ferry to Cormorant Island and Alert Bay.

The further north I go, the more wild and beautiful it becomes.
Shorelines sweep up to the road, with island and mountain
backdrops, only to be curtained off again by a canyon of fir trees.
There are wild lupins on the verges and road signs warn of logging
lorries and elk. I see my first bald eagle — the tell-tale flash of
white tail soaring over the trees. We pass Mount Washington —
big and brown and rocky. A girl in the seat opposite tells me that
it's Vancouver Island's major ski resort, but they had no snow this
year and it opened for only a week. "It's crazy," she says. "What's
happening?"

The trees, the mountains and the cloudscapes make me want
to get out a paintbrush, words seem so inadequate. We cross wild
rivers choked with driftwood, lakes just glimpsed between pine
trees like pieces of broken glass, white-capped peaks in the far
distance. There are more shades of green than there are letters
in the alphabet. But this is just a memory of the Great Forest
that once stretched from Siberia to Caledonia and beyond, across

America, Europe and Russia, one tree talking to another across the distances, root and branch. The wind could blow across the entire world without touching the ground.

The road through the forest

The journey takes nine hours and I get short glimpses of coastal holiday resorts like Qualicum, and have coffee in the beautiful Campbell River. Nanaimo, once the centre of a mining community, seems more commercial and connects ferries to a number of different locations. I could go from here south to Vancouver or the most northerly port of Prince Rupert, or get transport across the island to the Pacific Coast at Ucluelet, but for now it's just five minutes to stretch the legs and then back on the highway.

Along the road, telegraph poles, like twentieth century totems, signal lines of power connecting settlement to settlement, here and there encroaching on the tide of green, as we push further and further north. Clear-cut logging creates bald patches like some kind of plague — other areas are burn-back brown after wild-fires. Up dirt tracks that intersect the highway, there are plumes of dust whirled up by the wind, following the progress of invisible logging trucks. At our brief stops the air smells different, of pine resin, bitter earth, hot tarmac and, underneath, a base note of salt from the Pacific

As I get off the bus in Port McNeill there's a dark-skinned little boy, with tightly curled hair and very bright eyes, waiting at the bottom of the steps. He looks about eight years old.

"Where you going?" he asks.

I'm puzzled, but answer, "The ferry terminal."

"Where to?"

"Alert Bay."

He catches hold of my arm and tells me to come with him. I'm a bit wary, not used to being kidnapped, but he pulls me over to a taxi parked next to the bus. An elderly man is leaning against the wall in the shade. He's slim and small — shorter than me — and has a beard and faded, but still twinkly, blue eyes. He's wearing a cowboy hat, checked shirt and denims. "You going to Alert Bay?" he asks as he comes forward. Close-to, he's a lot older than he'd seemed at first glance. I tell him I am, but that I don't know what time the ferry goes.

He points out across the town to the harbour and a white dot approaching. "That's the one you want." He has a strange accent, with very soft consonants.

"Can I walk?" I'm still desperately trying to watch the dollars. "How far's the terminal?"

"You haven't got time. Ferry's due in ten minutes."

The little boy, who seems to be called Billy, opens the car door and the taxi driver insists on lifting my luggage into the boot, although I fear for his health, but I'm made totally aware that it would be the height of rudeness to insist on lifting it myself. In the taxi he tells me that his name is Jean-Paul, though everyone calls him Jack. It's the only question I'm allowed to ask. He quizzes me all the way about who I am and where I've come from, where I'm going and why.

I tell him I'm on holiday from England.

He's scrutinising me carefully out of the corner of his eye as he drives and tells me that he's a great reader of character. He thinks I'm a teacher (almost right there) and that I write things (this man is psychic?). Apparently he has a friend who is a writer who comes every summer. I reluctantly admit my occupation. Jack volunteers some information about himself. He came to do logging here as a young man, was offered a permanent job and stayed. He's supposed to be retired now, and sold his taxi business years ago but the person who bought it didn't run it properly (by his standards), so he took it back.

It's only a short distance to the ferry terminal, but he's right, I couldn't have walked it in time. Cars are already streaming off the boat when we arrive. Jack parks at the door of the ticket office and comes inside with me to make sure I get the right ticket. Then he gives me his card and says I have to telephone him when I come back and he'll be waiting. He says goodbye and waves me off like an old friend.

Inter-island Ferry, British Columbia

The ferry is small — there are only about a dozen cars. The crew have it turned round and on its way again in less than fifteen minutes, churning out into the strait towards distant islands — one of them mine. I stand at the rail watching a hummock of green slowly draw nearer. It feels good to be out in the fresh sea air after so many hours on the bus. A member of the crew finishes coiling the mooring rope and tells me that orca were seen in the bay last night. My heart beats faster. What I would give to see orca here. "It's paradise over there," the man says, nodding his head towards the shore. "A little paradise."

Cormorant Island isn't very big, about three miles from one end to the other. It's shaped rather like a comma, with the only settlement, Alert Bay, in the centre of the curve, facing Vancouver Island. I've seen photographs and paintings. Emily Carr came here more than once on her sketching expeditions and the totems and war canoes along the shoreline became a favourite subject for her. I've been re-reading her notebooks and journals as part of the research for my visit. I also looked at quite a lot of artefacts and their history in the Museum of Anthropology in Vancouver. This area of British Columbia forms the traditional lands of the Kwakwaka'wakw people, one of the Haida Nation's closest neighbours, and Cormorant Island is home to the 'Namgis Band. Their welcome, in the Kwakwala language, is carved on a cross beam as you walk off the boat. I don't have a map of Alert Bay, but I know that my accommodation is along the sea front, so I just turn right and walk. Sure enough, about five minutes from the ferry, there's a building that looks like the image I saw on the internet.

The Seine Boat Inn

The Seine Boat Inn is a house built out over the beach on

stilts. Like the other waterfront buildings, it has its feet in the sea. The ale yellow paint looks slightly shabby on the outside after the onslaught of winter weather, but it has a lot of character and there's a London black cab, parked in a terminal position, on the gravel outside. Inside, the rooms are immaculate and beautifully decorated. I have two queen beds with feather quilts and a mountain of white pillows. I also have a fully equipped kitchen and a bathroom to dream about. Doors open on each side onto wooden walkways where I can sit and stare out to sea. I open the windows and let the salty air blow through. It's very nice not to be moving after so many hours either on a bus or a boat.

Alert Bay is really off the track. I ask the motel owner about food and learn that the General Store is closed (things close early here) and there are only a couple of eateries open at this time of year. There's a diner just along the street which is okay, and a small restaurant further down, but that's expensive and 'you can wait a long time'. They, too, close early. I'm seriously hungry, so I head for the diner.

I hadn't imagined anything so basic; rather like a school canteen with plastic tables and chairs. The floor is littered with the debris of previous customers; dropped napkins, straws and ring pulls and the tables that have been cleared have a smear of grease. I hesitate for a moment, but then remember that there's only one other alternative that didn't get much of a recommendation, so I sit down. Two people come in behind me. I'd seen them on the boat, riding a powerful motorbike. They look English and when I hear them talking to each other they have strong English accents. They're hesitating too. I ask where they're from and they tell me they're from Birmingham on a motorcycle tour of British Columbia, having a fantastic time. They decide they're going to risk the diner too.

An Asian woman comes out of the kitchen and asks what I want to drink. There isn't a lot of choice. I don't like beer and don't fancy Sprite or Coca Cola, so I ask if there's any wine. She answers that they have white wine or red wine, but she doesn't know what kind of wine it is. I mentally strangle my middle-class doppelganger but order it anyway. The red wine is poured from a carton, comes in a half-pint glass and tastes like something you could put on chips. If you want to get out into the wild it's no use expecting a Jamie Oliver's in every hamlet. But I'm beginning to realise that my privileged western lifestyle has conditioned my expectations. I want to experience the wild, but I also want the creature comforts I've become accustomed, perhaps addicted, to; the very things that are going to have to go if we're going to be saved from ourselves. A sentence from an article I've just read, by Kathleen Jamie, comes into my head, about educated, middle class people on spiritual quests. I suddenly like myself rather less than I did when I arrived.

An elderly man is sitting at a table in the corner watching the TV. The Black Hawks are playing the Ducks again, the score is 3-2 and, from his body language and exclamations, it's obviously very exciting. The woman comes out of the kitchen and says something in an angry voice. She seems completely phased because there are three people wanting to order food at the same time. The man gets up reluctantly, fetches a pad from the counter and comes to take our orders. His English is very basic and I'm not sure he understands. I try to make it simple by ordering today's special off the board. The couple from Birmingham are being more ambitious.

My butter chicken, when it comes, is the shade of orange you only see on high-viz jackets or traffic cones, but there are two garlic pitta breads and it tastes welcome to someone who hasn't eaten all day, though once my hunger has worn off I stop eating. The couple at the next table aren't so lucky and don't get the meal they ordered from the menu. There are loud voices in the kitchen. The bill, when it comes, is seriously unwelcome. My dish of butter chicken (which I couldn't finish) and glass of wine (ditto) costs more than any meal I had in either Vancouver or Victoria, so it's down to the shop tomorrow morning to buy some supplies. I don't think either my digestive system or my bank account could cope with another evening in the diner.

Afterwards, I walk along the edge of the island towards the old 'Namgis burial ground. The carved poles slant in different directions on the sloping grass facing the sea. Some are leaning precipitously, one or two have fallen and are in an advanced state of decay, others are freshly painted and clearly new. Unlike our own culture, the First Nation people believe that 'everything has its day, nothing lasts for ever', so the totems are not maintained. They are allowed to fall and rot and new ones are erected when someone else dies. Death and decay are part of the cycle of life. There's a notice asking people to respect the dead and not to walk on the field. I take photographs from the road. A big, wooden building, shuttered and empty, stands next to the burial ground. This, my information leaflet tells me, is the old nurses' home. The hospital it served, behind the cemetery, is now gone.

The Namgis burial ground with totem.

The evenings are long so far north and it's not dark until late. I walk on round the bay before I go to bed. It's rather forlorn. There are boats under tarpaulins drawn up high on the edge of the road. Wooden houses that look like holiday homes are shuttered tight with a whole winter's worth of wind debris drifted up on the porch. There are cafés and shops, even a pub. Most have signs in the window saying 'Closed for Winter' and some have 'For Sale' signs too. Everything needs repair and a coat of paint. This doesn't feel like a thriving community, more like one clinging on by its fingernails. If this is paradise, it's paradise in decline. I wonder about the young people. How do they make a living here?

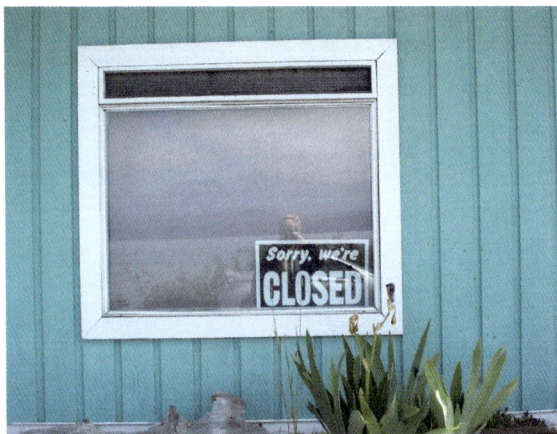

Closed for Winter

Back at the Inn I leave my window open and fall asleep listening to the sea. I'm a little bothered by the lights of the ferry, which docks at ten thirty and apparently stays here all night ready for the six thirty run in the morning — an early start I will have to make at the end of the week.

7. The Legend of Siwidis

'When one's heart is glad, one gives away gifts.'
Grandmother Agnes Alfred, Community Leader, Alert Bay

After the experience of the diner last night, I visit the General Store this morning as soon as I get up. So now I have rice and porridge and coffee and bread and I won't starve. It really is a one-stop shop, selling everything from furniture and white goods to clothes, stationary and food, though I was surprised by the number of aisles dedicated to fizzy drinks and different types of salted snack. Afterwards I sit on the seat on my balcony and drink a large mug of very good Canadian coffee, accompanied by a stack of toast, looking out across the bay. Still not an orca in sight.

After breakfast I wander along the seafront in the opposite direction to the one I took last night. Alert Bay is in two halves; the European half and the First Nation half. It's a legacy of apartheid, the original policy of putting the indigenous population in reservations. But not everything could be divided tidily. The traditional burial ground is in the European sector. This morning I'm heading into the old reservation to visit what is called the U'mista Centre, which, I've been told, is a museum and a wonderful cultural experience.

I walk along the shoreline, towards U'mista, which I can see clearly from the other side of the bay. It's constructed like a traditional 'Bighouse', with long beams, a sloping roof and wide front. The front is painted white and decorated in black with the symbols of the 'Namgis Nation. At the bottom is a killer whale, and above it, as if perched on the whale's back, the spreading wings of the mythical Thunderbird. It's a modern version of the historic 'Namgis Chief Tlakwudlas' Big House built in 1873 which appears in old photographs of Alert Bay. I've looked at as many of these as I could find. There's also a diorama at the Wisconsin Public Museum, available online, that shows, in colour, what the seafront once looked like, with the Chief's house in the foreground.[21]

Umista Cultural Centre, Alert Bay.

The ordinary houses I pass on the right hand side of the road are either double or single-storey wooden structures with verandas and porches, painted in pastel colours. Modest houses. There are three double decker buses parked on a grassy lot. One offers a tour of London, another is going to Morecambe Bay in Cumbria, not far from my own home. I wonder who has brought them here, across such huge distances, but there are several English people on Cormorant Island, including my host at the Seine Boat Inn.

The current chief of the 'Namgis has a brightly painted totem pole outside the house. It features a killer whale with a man on its back. This reminds me of the Maori legend of Paikea riding from the Pacific Islands to New Zealand on the back of a whale. Like the southern Pacific Maori, the northern Pacific Kwakwaka'wakw were also whale people, who skilfully pursued whales for food in long canoes with a notched prow to rest the harpoon on. Alert Bay is still a favourite location for sightings of Orca, from June to October. But today, the sea is flat calm, glittering in the sun, with no sign of any wildlife out there at all.

"End of the road"

On the seaward side of the road, fishing boats are corralled in the shelter of a marina. Fishing has always been an integral part of life here. There are big Seine boats, small clinker built crabbing boats, and sleek gin palaces with supports for line fishing. Some of them look as if they haven't been to sea in a while. The shoreline is dominated by a derelict salmon canning factory, in a picturesque state of decay, on stilts out into the bay. Apparently it was one of the area's biggest employers, but there just aren't enough salmon to make it pay anymore.

As I walk, seagulls shriek overhead and bald eagles circle and swoop from the treetops. There's a notice on the lamp posts along the shore warning that it's forbidden to fish for mussels, oysters and clams because of contamination and the risk of Paralytic Shellfish Poisoning for anyone who eats them. These bi-valve filter feeders are infected by neurotoxins from algal blooms out in the ocean — once a rare occurrence, but becoming more frequent and just another small sign of an ecosystem under stress. This disease has always existed (Vancouver's ship lost a crewman to it) but it is now increasing with the frequency of algal blooms. It's not just human beings that are at risk, it also decimates all the mammals that live on bi-valves — like the sea-otters.

Fishing boat setting off from Alert Bay

U'mista has been built next to where the biggest and most infamous of the residential schools, St Michael's, was erected by the government in 1929 and which replaced an earlier school built in the nineteenth century. St Michael's was run by the Anglican Church and held around two hundred children from communities on Vancouver Island as far south as Campbell River, as well as First Nation children from Haida Gwaii, and northern mainland communities from Bella Bella, Bella Coola and Prince Rupert. Kwakwaka'wakw, Haida, Nisga'a and Heiltsuk children were all educated together here, far from their own families and communities. TB sufferers were also quarantined in the same building with the children. Not surprisingly, there was a high death rate. But at least, as far as the authorities were concerned, they died as Christians and little Canadians. The Missionary

Society of the Church of England reported in 1934 that they thanked 'Almighty God for what has been accomplished: for a race of people brought in the shortest period of time known in history from the most debasing savagery to citizenship both in the Kingdom of our God and in his God-blessed Dominion of Canada.'[22]

I had expected to see the building, a formidable presence in the photographs I'd looked at, but all I find is an expanse of newly seeded, bare earth. St Michael's Residential School has been razed to the ground. I ask the man in the museum what has happened and he tells me that the building was given back to the 'Namgis after it closed, as part of the Truth and Reconciliation process. There had been a great deal of debate and an attempt to use the building for business purposes, but finally it was decided that, after a cleansing ceremony, it would be demolished. The memories it generated were just too terrible to live with. The bulldozers had moved in only a couple of months ago and the ground is now being re-planted and will be allowed to heal.

In U'mista, you can read the stories of individual survivors. Some of them are heroic. George Quocksister and his younger brother Louis were orphans from Campbell River when they were sent to St Michael's. They plotted to escape, stole a rowing boat and rowed to Kelsey Bay on Vancouver Island, several hours down the Johnstone Strait towards their home in Campbell River. George said he had such terrible blisters on his hands that he could hardly bear the pain, but he was determined to get away. He was lucky, because many children died trying to escape.

George and his brother were later discovered and sent to another school in Port Alberni, deep in the interior, a remote location on an inlet from the Pacific west coast of Vancouver Island. The nearest place was Nanaimo, a rough trek through difficult terrain. The Indian agent who left them there said, "Now try to escape!" but George managed to get them out and back to Campbell River again. This time he was caught and taken before a judge, but he argued that he could support himself by fishing and was allowed to remain free. George married and had nine children of his own and wouldn't allow any of them to go to the residential schools, even under threat of imprisonment. One of his daughters said that, "When the Indian agent came, my dad told him if he touched a hair on any of our heads, he would blow him away with his shotgun." Through his rebellion, George managed to hang on to his language and culture and was able to pass it on to his children.[23]

U'mista means 'that which has been given back' and it was originally applied to the ransom of clan members kidnapped into slavery by another tribe, or the repossession of belongings taken in an enemy raid. It is a very appropriate word for the contents of the museum, which have been returned to the 'Namgis Nation from museums and private collections around the world. Many of the heritage objects, masks and sacred regalia in U'mista were seized after what is referred to as the Christmas Raid of 1921, when police and Indian Agents raided a Potlatch being given by 'Namgis Chief Dan Cranmer.

The Potlatch has always been a central part of First Nation culture, celebrating birth, death, marriage, the creation of a new Chief, or any other significant occasion, and also a key element of their legal and political structure. In an oral culture it was important that any agreements or events were witnessed by as many people as possible to prevent disputes. It was traditional for the Chief to give gifts to all the guests at the Potlatch, so it was also a way of distributing wealth. A Chief who was rich and successful would Potlatch many times, enriching all his people. But it was also a celebration. As one Elder puts it today: 'When one's heart is glad, one gives away gifts. It was given to us by our Creator, to be our way of doing things, to be our way of rejoicing, we who are Indian. The Potlatch was given to us to be our way of expressing joy.'[24]

It was an occasion for storytelling, dancing and music, so that it kept alive the clan's culture and traditions. Because of this, Potlatching was seen as a big threat to the colonisers and it was banned by the Indian Act of 1884. It was believed to be an obstacle to 'civilising the savages' as well as 'a waste of resources materially and financially' because it 'also removed a large amount of the workforce from canneries and fisheries during the winter months'[25] One missionary believed that the whole point of the Potlatch was notoriety. 'Their evil lies in the fact that a man will give away his "all" for the sake of gaining a name.'[26] Anyone caught participating in a Potlatch could be imprisoned for up to six months. But it was so central to First Nation culture that they carried on, in secret locations, often subverting the Indian Act by disguising the celebrations as christening or wedding parties. The Kwakwaka'wakw people occupied a substantial territory on several islands, so it was easier for them to carry on the tradition, concealed from church and state officials, in remote locations as they moved from their summer to their winter villages. But in 1921, their luck ran out.

Chief Dan Cranmer held a Potlatch on the remote Village Island and hundreds of people attended, among them informants who gave away the date and the location to government agents and the Royal Canadian Mounted Police. There was a raid, all the ceremonial regalia was seized, and those arrested were tried in Vancouver a couple of months later. '49 Kwakwaka'wakw individuals were convicted for potlatch activities, some simply for dancing; 22 were arrested and sentenced to two months in prison; four were sentenced to six months.' Others were given suspended sentences 'after agreeing to stop potlatching and relinquish their ceremonial regalia.'

This was particularly significant. Over four hundred pieces had been seized, under Section 149 of the Indian Act, and they found their way into museums.[27] There was a big demand for Canadian ethnographical and anthropological material in Britain and America at the time. Europeans believed that First Nation culture was disappearing and would soon be gone forever. Several expeditions were mounted to collect artefacts for museums. Franz Boas, an anthropologist from Columbia University, who had been a curator for the Smithsonian, instructed his student, John Swanton, in a letter to bring back as many 'masks, totem poles, memorial poles, grave posts, painted blankets, shamans' staffs, horn spoons' and other regalia, as he could.[28]

There was 'stiff competition between museum collectors to create the most comprehensive collection in their museum'.[29] This passion for collecting not only ignored the rights of ownership of the people they belonged to, but also the spiritual and cultural significance of the objects themselves. A lot of energy and legal expertise is now having to be devoted to getting the stolen property back to its original owners. In 1967, the Kwakwaka'wakw began the process of recovering the regalia seized in 1921. They have had some success, over four decades, and it has inspired others, but for many First Nation people precious objects, including human body parts, still languish in foreign museums and private collections.

In England the Pitt Rivers Museum in Oxford is only one of a number of organisations that still have a big anthropological collection of British Columbian artefacts, which were removed — often under dubious circumstances — from their owners, though this continues to be a very sensitive and controversial subject. Lt General Augustus Henry Lane-Fox Pitt Rivers was a nineteenth century aristocrat and landowner, the nephew of the 17th Earl of Morton, with a great interest in ethnography and archaeology. He was a typical 'gentleman amateur' of his day, with all the convictions and prejudices of his class and upbringing. Pitt Rivers was influenced by the writings of Charles Darwin and Herbert Spencer. He amassed a huge collection of aboriginal artefacts to support his own theories of cultural evolution, and wanted them, when displayed, to illustrate, 'the successive ideas by which the minds of men in a primitive condition of culture have progressed in the development of their arts from the simple to the complex, and from the homogeneous to the heterogeneous.'[30] He endowed the Museum to house his collection in 1884, fifteen years before he died.

As instructed by the staff, I enter the big hall of the U'mista museum anti-clockwise, as everyone who wanted to enter the spirit-world did in First Nation cultures. In Europe it's referred to as Widdershins, going 'in a direction contrary to the apparent course of the sun' and it has deep significance. It is the 'left hand way' of spiritual (and often female) knowledge in Celtic mythology. European Christianity abhorred it and declared it unlucky.

The masks and robes are on open display, so there's no glass between you and the objects, and they're arranged in the order each one would appear in the Potlatch dance, as the story unfolds. Apart from the masks there are drums, spruce root hats and the carved chests once used to store the regalia. There are headdresses that were worn by chiefs and shamans, made from carved wood and decorated with abalone shell, white eagle down and ermine tails. Some of the masks are now over a hundred years old and very fragile. Animal skin and hair still clings to the carved wood, but the once vibrant colours have faded. They have a grace and dignity I didn't expect. Words written by a previous visitor resonate; 'There is a real sense of power and greatness that emanates from the collection.'[31]

Each artefact still belongs to the family it was taken from and they have the right to 'borrow' the regalia for their own important ceremonies. The re-establishment of the Potlatch is at the heart of contemporary First Nation culture. The part of the Indian Act forbidding it wasn't repealed until 1951, and by then there were few still alive who could remember what the ceremonies were. But it was considered so important that the remaining traditional Chiefs began to Potlatch straight away so that the young people could learn the stories and the dances. One of these, particular to the 'Namgis people, is the story of Siwidis. When I visited the Bill Reid Gallery I was able to watch a video of a very important Potlatch ceremony here at Alert Bay in 1987, and look at the masks that had been carved for the re-enactment of this story by a number of contemporary First Nation artists including Beau Dick, who is also a traditional Chief of the Kwakwaka'wakw.

The masks represent transformation, from animal to human to supernatural being. By putting on the skin of an animal you could become that animal, because under the skin we are the same. Most First Nation languages have no word for Nature because they do not see it as something separate from themselves. We are part of it and we shape-shift through the natural universe as our atoms take on different forms. The masks represent this. Some of them are hinged transformation masks; one of them is a gigantic fish, the bottom-dwelling Sculpin, which then opens to reveal a bird's beak which opens in turn to reveal a human face. In the story of Siwidis, he undergoes many transformations.'

The story of Siwidis, mask, Umista Museum, Alert Bay

Just entering one of the 'Bighouses' where the chiefs potlatched, was a spiritual experience. In Kwakwaka'wakw territory, the house pole at the front has an opening which is the entrance to the house. It's small, so that you have to duck down to get in, but this is defensive, protecting the occupants from enemies. Sometimes the entrance hole is carved as the mouth of an animal, or the beak of a raven. In the latter case, the lower beak would be pulled down and used as a staircase to gain entry. A house is more than just a building, it is a living thing with links to the ancestors. When a new 'Bighouse' was built in Alert Bay and the chief, Jimmy Sewid, held the Potlatch there in 1987, he explained to one of the invited guests that, 'The door of the house is the mouth of our ancestor. It is the mouth of heaven. The fire is the soul of the house'. Inside the Bighouse, his guest, a hereditary chief of the Kwaigu'i First Nation, said that he 'looked up and saw the backbone, ribs, and soul. I could feel it, sense it, and touch it with my spirit.'[32]

Imagine yourself in the Bighouse, among the guests crowded around the perimeter, crouched on the ground, the only source of light a fire in the middle of the floor. The air is thick with smoke. The musicians are shaking rattles and beating sticks on wooden log drums, creating an intense, hypnotic rhythm for the dance, while voices chant above you. Siwidis enters in his human form. He is feeling suicidal after being expelled from his village for dishonour. As he stands on the edge of the sea, wondering whether to drown himself, an Octopus appears and drags him down into the underwater realm where he meets Komugwe, the Chief Under the Sea. This under-the-sea kingdom is a mirror image of the kingdom over ground. There is a Raven figure and an Eagle figure and D'Sonoquis — the Wild Woman of the Sea. The dancing figures, masked and robed, act out the story in the flickering firelight, which projects strange shadows. The chanting and percussion induce a trance-like state, and a suspension of belief. Some of the looming figures, made taller by the wooden structures of the masks, seem threatening and dangerous.

Siwidis has surprising courage, passes all the challenges, is given the gift of transformation, becomes a shaman, and joins the dance with other creatures of the underwater world, the Starfish, the Sea Lion, the Sea Otter and the Sea Grizzly — which is a strange hybrid, part fish, part bear. Siwidis gains other powers, puts on other masks and he returns to the surface as a whale with an eagle on his dorsal fin, then transforms into a Sculpin, and finally into a human being again. He returns to his village and becomes the leader of his people. The story of Siwidis's journey will be carved on the pole that is erected outside his house. It belongs to him and to his descendants forever.

The music fades into silence. The masks are removed, the robes folded back into their carved chests. The fire dies down.

When you come from the dark into the light, there's a real sense of having been into another world.

8. Beside the Singing Forest

'[Her] fixed stare bored into me as if the very life of the old cedar looked out, and it seemed that the voice of the tree itself might have burst from the great round cavity … that was her mouth.'
Emily Carr, *Klee Wyck*

The weather is still hot, with blue, cloudless skies and calm seas. It's cool in the morning and again in the evening, but by noon the heat has really begun to build. On the mainland the strawberries are ripening weeks earlier than usual and wildfires are now burning at several locations. Today I'm going to try to walk round the island, using the beach and forest trails, keeping in the shade as much as possible. The woman who runs the small library that doubles as exhibition centre and tourist information has given me a simple map and some directions and told me to be very careful to watch the tide.

Harbour view, Alert Bay

As I set out along the bay, several bald eagles are wheeling overhead and there's an 'unkindness of ravens' sitting on the rooftop of a nearby house. It seems very unkind to give such an intelligent bird such a malevolent collective name. Although they are corvids, ravens are not 'large crows' as some people think. They are quite different; big, black, inquisitive, cunning, and extremely beautiful. They are the tricksters of the bird-world, able to figure out how to do all kinds of things and also able to use tools. Ravens have captured the human imagination for thousands of years and appear in a number of mythologies. In Haida the raven is the most intelligent, the trickster — one to watch out for. The god Odin in Norse mythology had two ravens perched on his shoulders. Bran the Blessed, the Celt, won battles through the intervention of the ravens and it is due to him that ravens protect the Tower of London. There's a legend that if the ravens ever leave, the kingdom will fall. In the epic of Gilgamesh, which echoes the story of Noah in Genesis, a dove, a swallow and a raven are sent out to check if the water has receded after the ark has lodged on the mountain. The first two return but the raven does not and so they know that, somewhere, there is dry land. In Haida mythology it is the raven himself who pulls the land up out of the flood-water.

I am trying to take some pictures of a pair of ravens, who are eyeing me curiously from the beach, when an elderly 'Namgis woman stops to talk to me. She is pushing her mother in a wheelchair and glad of a rest. She asks if I would like my photo taken with the ravens. I tell her I really like them and she seems amused by my fascination. She laughs and says, "It's probably because they are mischievous. Just like you!" This, from someone who has only just met me. Obviously it must be something in the eyes.

As I walk on round the bay, there's a little wooden church painted white with a steeply pitched roof and a picket fence, just like the church in one of Emily Carr's paintings. I stop to take a photograph. It tells its own story of the nineteenth century religious motivation behind a large part of the colonial agenda and the involvement of the church in carrying out government policy. Church and State worked together. As the infamous McKenna-McBride Commission stated in 1913, 'Christianity and Western Civilization have always gone hand in hand.'[33] To the establishment, all indigenous people were 'savages' and it was your Christian duty to convert them by any means possible, turning them into useful cogs in the capitalist wheel.

Church, Alert Bay

The Catholics, the Anglicans and the Free Church competed for souls. In *Klee Wyck*, Emily Carr describes a pair of female missionaries at Ucluelet as they struggle to establish a mission school and encourage people to come to church by blowing a large cow horn to summon them to prayer. They aren't attractive characters. The two women she calls 'Lesser' and 'Greater', have no sense of humour and little sympathy for the people they are trying to convert, communicating with them, not in their own language, but using a pidgin dialect called Chinook. They are typical of the many women who came from Europe to the New World to escape the strait-jacket of Victorian society. Being a missionary was one of the options open to ambitious, adventurous, religious women in search of a fulfilling career at a time when other positions in the church were closed to them. But the basic Christian values of compassion and charity seem to have been lacking in their dealings with First Nation culture.

You can get insights into the mind-set of these missionaries by reading some of their letters and diaries. The story of Emma Crosby, a Methodist missionary, is suitably titled *Good Intentions Gone Awry*. Emma married a Methodist minister who needed a wife, with the express intention of coming to British Columbia and converting the aboriginal people in the eighteen seventies. She and her husband were sent to Port Simpson, on the mainland, across the water from Haida Gwaii, almost on the border with Alaska. Emma set out to show, by example, what an ideal Christian wife should be, taking Tsimshian girls into her home to train them, though in practice this meant that they did the housework and looked after her children. Initially these girls lived 'en famille' as part of their training, helping Emma with her growing family, but it had an unforeseen result. The 'little children learned to talk Indian before they could speak English'. When Emma's daughters began speaking Tsimshian and telling stories that the girls had taught them, the experiment came to an end; integration and assimilation were only ever going to be one way. Emma set up one of the first residential schools with a rigid programme of education and social segregation. 'We do everything by rule. We have bedroom, dining-room, kitchen and wash-room rules, also general rules, or a time-table giving the hour for everything, from the rising-bell to bed-time.'[34] Children who were used to a nomadic family lifestyle in the open air were now incarcerated in an institution whose description as a 'home' was the most barbaric misnomer.

Margaret Butcher was a missionary nurse who came to

Kitamaat, a settlement on an inlet further south, in 1916. One of her jobs was to look after the physical welfare of the Haisla children in the residential school there. She thought the Haisla lazy; brought up to live by the mechanical clock she had no conception of a society that lived by the natural clock of the weather, the tide, and the seasons. She despised her charges, describing them as 'a slow, indolent, dirty people, bound very strongly by custom and superstition'.[35] The fact that the children were forgetting their native languages and learning hymns was considered progress and the death of one of the Elders something to be celebrated. There was little hope of complete Christianization until 'some half dozen of the old folks of the Village, who still hold fast to their ancient customs, are dead… each old person's death aids advancement.'[36]

Margaret was neither cruel nor unintelligent and genuinely believed that what she was doing was worth the pain she both suffered and inflicted. 'Oh, it is a grand work we are engaged in!' she wrote to her sister. 'There is a delight in it that is beyond anything I know.'[37] She spent three lonely years enduring personal privation, while policing the children's manners, morals and sexuality, which included keeping a strict record of her charges' menstrual cycles. Her comments hint at the abuses the indigenous people were subjected to. 'The white-man is not to be trusted when an Indian woman is around… an Indian woman is a white-man's tool.'[38] She presided over fatal epidemics of TB, Whooping Cough and the Spanish Flu that spread across the world in 1918. In one of her letters, twenty-nine of the thirty children in the school were seriously ill. Many did not survive. The death toll increased the animosity shown towards the school and the staff, which Margaret thought was very unfair: '… the Indians are so illogical, they do not consider the number of children who are brought through … to strength & fitness, they only look at & count the children who are sick & "are killed by the Home".'[39] Partly for this reason, children were often sent home to die, taking the infections to villages that had previously been clear. Tuberculosis, in particular, spread easily within the confines of the school and was exported to the villages. 'If a child shews definite signs of TB he must go.'[40] Margaret, in her letters, doesn't question anything and seems to have felt that she was always doing her Christian duty to convert 'the heathen'.

As one recent commentator has observed, both Emma and Margaret were 'highly intelligent, immensely competent, and profoundly toxic to the people they were trying to save.' But the same author also asks a very disturbing question. 'When future generations read our accounts about all the good we're doing in the world, will they regard us too as toxic and self-deluded fools?'[41] Consumer Capitalism is the religion that we are currently imposing on a large part of the 'developing' world, in the disguise of 'Aid', and I suspect that its effects are as toxic as anything inflicted by the missionaries of the past.

As I'm walking along the grit road thinking about all this, passing U'mista and the green expanse that used to be St Michaels, and looking up at the wooded hill rising up in the centre of the island, suddenly I meet my first 'wild' D'Sonoqua.

It was in Alert Bay that Emily Carr met D'Sonoqua, quite by accident. She was exploring the ruins of the houses and the old board-walks concealed by wild vegetation. She slipped on the damp wood, skidded to the base of a pole among the nettles and then looked up. There, staring down at her was a figure out of a nightmare:

'The great wooden image towering above me was indeed terrifying... Her head and trunk were carved out of, or rather into, the bole of a great red cedar. She seemed to be part of the tree itself, as if she had grown there at its heart, and the carver had only chipped away the outer wood so that you could see her. Her arms were spliced and socketed to the trunk, and were flung wide in a circling, compelling movement. Her breasts were two eagle-heads, fiercely carved... The eyes were two rounds of black, set in wider rounds of white, and placed in deep sockets under wide, black eyebrows. Their fixed stare bored into me as if the very life of the old cedar looked out, and it seemed that the voice of the tree itself might have burst from that great round cavity, with projecting lips, that was her mouth... The whole figure expressed power, weight, domination, rather than ferocity... I could scarcely wrench my eyes away from the clutch of

those empty sockets. The power that I felt was not in the thing itself, but in some tremendous force behind it, that the carver had believed in.' [42]

D'Sonoqua, Alert Bay

In Alert Bay, behind the U'mista centre, I too am confronted by D'Sonoqua. Black, with wide hollow eyes and red lips, breasts sucked dry and hanging down, she stares out to sea above my head. She is a symbol of fertility, but also of the destructive power of the natural world we are part of, that both gives and takes away and must never be taken for granted. The wild woman of the forest and under the sea reminds us of the wild landscape that is inside us, constrained by social conventions. I feel something of Emily Carr's sadness and longing when I look

91

at her; remembering all the things that I didn't do because I was afraid, or held back by social expectations. What could we do, what might we be capable of, if we went straight as an arrow for the truth?

As I walk up to join the forest trail, I pass the new Bighouse where the 1987 Potlatch was held. Outside is the tallest totem pole in the world, tapering up into the sky, too tall to photograph, like a giant antenna. Some boys are playing football on the grass outside.

The forest trail I've chosen turns out to be a 4-wheel drive track with numbered picnic places under the trees, some of them littered with rubbish and plastic bags. I persevere, thinking that when I get away from the beach, I will find the real forest, but when I get further in, the trail is blocked by fallen trees, several smashed and tangled, impossible to go through, over or around. Another trail becomes lost in undergrowth and I don't feel confident enough to go any further. It's easy to lose direction in dense woodland when you can't see either the sky or the sea. So I turn back again and retrace my steps. The woods are loud with the kronk of ravens, but there is no sense of being in the wild; civilisation with its rubbish, the sound of chainsaws and motor-boats, is always close.

The tide is low, but the beach is too hard to walk on; it's all pebbles and boulders and sea-and-sun-bleached tree trunks piled up by the winter storms. So I change the plan. Instead of doing a circumnavigation, I head inland for the high ground. The woman at the Tourist Information had told me about an ecological park, which the locals jokingly call 'Gator Gardens'. When they built the salmon canning plant, the owners had dammed the island's main freshwater spring to provide a water supply for the factory. One of the unanticipated results was that the forest at the summit of the island, where the spring rises, began to turn into a swamp, killing a lot of the trees and creating a new kind of environment. When the cannery closed the intention was to take the dam away and replant the trees, but so many people liked the swamp and so many animals and birds had colonised it, that the decision was made to keep it as a nature reserve.

Soon I'm walking on clearly marked trails through dense forest loud with birds. It's the salmonberry season and groups of red-breasted birds are picking at the bushes. A man in town has already told me that these are robins, but they are the size of thrushes and quite different to the English variety. The trees are draped in a type of lichen that hangs down, swinging in the breeze, called 'Witches' Hair'. Soon the ground becomes soggy underfoot and the trees begin to thin out, revealing skeletons of dead giants soaring up into the sky, the white ghosts of hemlocks and cedars with their roots in the water. Fortunately there's a network of boardwalks so that you can explore the swamp with dry feet.

I sit and eat my packed lunch on the edge of the walkway, dangling my legs above a pool that looks as if it could indeed have alligators in it. I'm the only person here. The forest around me echoes with the calls of kronking ravens, croaking crows, and woodpeckers tapping out morse code on the dead tree trunks. There's a blue heron perched on one of the bare, projecting branches. A pair of bald eagles circle overhead and there are other birds I don't recognise. Birds with dusky heads and bright pink breasts strut about, the size of blackbirds and with a distinctive call.

I lie down on the warm boards and look up at the sky. I could stay here forever; it's so peaceful. After a while, in this profound silence, you begin to notice even the smallest noises, such as the strange sound the ravens' wings make when they beat overhead, stroking the air like oars through water. When they glide, they're silent. In the water beside me, between the skunk cabbages, there are mysterious plops and drips.

My notebook is in my hand, full of scribbles, odd words and impressions. It seems impossible just to 'be'; I have to be forming images, turning everything into words, disciplining every experience into paragraphs. I'm beginning to realise that I see everything through the point of a pen.

After a while the sun begins to settle below the tree line. I get up and walk south, towards the southern tip of the island and soon I'm sitting at the end of the island on a rock, watching a bald eagle also perched on a rock further down. He or she is keeping a very close eye on me. The sea is mirror calm and the distant islands look near enough to swim to. A fleet of sea birds are dipping and surfacing in a kelp bed just off shore and on the eastern horizon there's a backdrop of tall, snow-tipped mountains.

The Inner Passage, Cormorant Island

I can feel myself winding down to a slower pace for the first time since I arrived.

9. Port McNeill — Billy and Jean-Paul

'The conquest of the earth, which mostly means the taking it away from those who have a different complexion or slightly flatter noses than ourselves, is not a pretty thing when you look into it too much.'
Joseph Conrad, *Heart of Darkness*

Don't mention the restrictions on seal hunting here — seals are the "pesky critters that eat the fish we need to catch in order to make a living". But seals might need to eat too? "Not our fish!" The fact that we can eat almost anything and seals can't, doesn't sway any arguments here. There's only fishing as a means of making a living on the island and seal-skins still fetch a hefty price. Tourism comes way down the list of lucrative enterprises. The mental attitudes of people who rely on fish for a living haven't changed much since the fishery patrol vessels were equipped with machine guns to slaughter sea lions and seals in the nineteen twenties. Mercifully, that doesn't happen any more, but the mindset remains the same in a high percentage of the population. It's not climate change or human activity that has depleted the fish stocks, it's our competitors in the ocean. The vast majority of the indigenous population think differently.

I'm sitting on a seat outside the ferry office, awake early, with another forty five minutes before the ferry leaves, but there are a few other early birds here happy to have a conversation. Everyone wants to talk — people in shops, people in their front gardens as you walk past — newcomers are curiosities, they all want to know where you've come from and what you're doing. Right now I'm having a conversation with a middle-aged woman whose husband is a fisherman. She comes from Nanaimo, but has been here for ten years. When it comes to wildlife versus humans she knows exactly which side she's on.

It's not just the preservation of seals that is contentious in the local community. The 'Namgis people are very active in protecting their own natural resources against the 'ever increasing corporate and industrial exploitation' of a capitalist economy. Their hereditary Chief, Bill Cranmer, son of the famous Potlatch giver Dan Cranmer, warns of an environmental crisis. 'As the years go by there are fewer trees, fewer fish, our land is being alienated.'[43] Keen to establish international links, the 'Namgis gave a ceremonial welcome to Greenpeace in 2004 and joined them in a protest against commercial salmon farming, which they believe is one of the factors in the decline of wild salmon stocks.[44] They are worrying about the side effects of fish farming; sea lice, the pollution of the clam beds on the beaches, 'destruction of seafloor ecosystems', as well as predator control mechanisms that adversely affect other marine animals including Orca.[45] I've been made aware that the revival of First Nation culture and the restitution of their rights isn't going down well with everyone. "Political correctness gone mad" was one observation. "Why can't they just get over it and get on with it like the rest of us?" Two of the people who expressed reservations to me were actually immigrants who had come to Canada from England or America. They had no sense that they were in someone else's country and that some sensitivity might be appropriate. They were used to being in charge. They worked hard and felt that they deserved what they had. There was a definite sense of entitlement.

There's a big contingent of high school children on the 6.30am ferry. When we dock in Port McNeill there's still an hour and a half until school begins, so the kids hang out in the harbour café drinking smoothies and hot chocolate. I order a coffee to take out, stand on the step for one last look at the islands and then turn my back to walk up to the bus depot. There's an hour to kill until my bus comes in, but the café is too crowded and noisy.

As I arrive I see two familiar figures sitting on a concrete bench outside. Billy and Jean-Paul aka Jack. They stand up as soon as

96

"Riding the Dog"

they see me walking up and Jack gets a key out of his pocket and opens the office door. Billy switches the computer on and asks me if I've got a ticket. He's quite disappointed to find that I have.

"He's a wizard with that computer," Jack says. "Me, I can't even turn one on!"

I ask Jack if he runs the bus depot as well as the taxi service, but he shakes his head. "The woman that does, she's had to go to her daughter, so she asked me to keep an eye on the place for her." He nods towards Billy, who is now selling tickets to a couple who've just come in, handling the credit card machine like a professional, "Now he's the one who does the business. He's real smart."

"How old is he?"

"Twelve. Just. His mom moved here from Toronto and he got bullied at school, so she took him out. He's home schooled."

I think he's getting a very different education to the one envisaged by the authorities, but it doesn't seem to be doing him any harm.

97

"Him and me, we're a bit the same," Jack goes on. "My parents were French, with a little farm in Alberta. I didn't speak a word of English when I went to school and I didn't get along all that well. There was a bakery I had to walk past every morning on the way to school and I used to stop and look in and one day when I was about thirteen I went in and asked if they had a job. And they had, so I took it. Every morning my Mom gave me my lunch and sent me off and I went to work and came home in the evening and never told them I'd been at the bakery. But they found out. I thought my Dad'd be mad as fire, but he just laughed and said, 'You made more grades than me, boy,' and so from then on, there was no more talk of school."

I ask him how he got from Alberta to here and he told me that he'd saved up his money from the bakery and then started work with a construction company that took him all over the state. He said that he'd watched men logging and thought, I could do that, and so he used his savings to buy a chainsaw — what he called 'a little machine'. "There weren't so many of them then," he explains.

By this time, his mother was dead, giving birth to his youngest sister and his father was raising the baby by himself.

"She went into labour on the farm and she knew the baby was coming wrong," Jack tells me. "So she walked down to the highway and got the bus into town. She was walking from the bus depot up to the hospital when she collapsed in the street. They managed to save the baby, but not her."

It's obvious that it's a difficult memory. I say I'm sorry.

"They were different times," Jack says.

He came to British Columbia logging and, because he had the 'little machine' and could work quickly, he was soon in demand. He explained to me that he had been a skilled 'faller', taking the trees down to very exact specifications. But some of the bosses weren't fussy. "Where do you want them?" he'd ask and the reply would be "Down! Just down." He and his team could fell more than a hundred of the giant redwoods in a single day. It gives me heartache just to think of it. One of those big cedars takes two hundred years to mature and the really big ones can be almost a thousand years old. When they go, a whole ecosystem goes with them. Now, Jack says, there aren't the old growth trees any more to satisfy demand, and the big money's gone out of it.

One of the questions I overheard people asking most often in Alert Bay was 'Have you got any work?' I ask Jack what else people earn money from around here. Fishing, he says. Though the fish are gone now too. The herring have to be protected and the salmon, which used to be so numerous there were tales of salmon runs where you could walk across the river on the backs of the fish, are elusive. "The million dollar catch used to be a regular thing," Jack tells me. "But not any more. Still, there are more millionaires round here than anywhere else in Canada."

I begin to suspect that Jack is one of them. He is what we call in the north of England a 'warm man', meaning there's enough in the bank account to keep out the winter chill. When Jack took me to the ferry on my first day, he'd pointed out his house on the bluff overlooking the strait, a sizable piece of real estate with fabulous views. Now he tells me how he got the land and how he built the house. Apart from the logging concessions, he's had a number of businesses; a removal van, a saw mill, various construction projects, the taxi service, still has financial fingers in a lot of proverbial pies, and he's just bought one of his granddaughters a house.

I'm trying to get a handle on how old he is, and the numbers keep stacking up. Much older than I'd thought at first. He was a late starter in the relationship business. When he met his wife she was in a refuge for victims of domestic abuse, with the children from her first marriage, and she was terrified of men. "How I ever got hooked up with her, I don't know," he says with a wry smile. But they had two more children and he's now a great grandfather. That's a lot of mileage, but there's still a quite a bit of tread on the tyres. He'll keep working until he dies. "What else is there to do?" he asks. Now tourism is becoming the business everyone relies on, particularly kayaking. "Elderly women," Jack says with a big grin. "Don't ask me why."

Another long bus journey and a ferry crossing, before getting on a plane for Haida Gwaii tomorrow. In the south, although the summer season hasn't officially begun yet and won't until June 18th, there is hay-timing in the fields and all the summer flowers are out; lupins and peonies and roses and rhododendrons. It seems odd that they don't count this as summer, particularly as temperatures are up in the high twenties. But everyone keeps telling me that this weather is unusual. The salmon berries are ripening two weeks early and other crops are also out of step with the season.

I fall through the door of my airport hotel at 10pm totally exhausted after my early start. I've been booked into room 911 with an excellent view of the runway, but I try not to let it worry me. I have another early start tomorrow, so I'm quickly into bed, though I can't resist having a peek at the international news before I go to sleep.

Canadian novelist Margaret Atwood is being interviewed on late night TV and she's talking about the Residential Schools, stating in a very forthright way that they were totally Dickensian. It wasn't just that they broke the links between the children and their communities, she explains, the children were never parented so that they never learned how to be parents themselves and their own children suffered. "Now," she says, "we're reaping the consequences." She talks about the imbalance of Native people in prison, homeless, or suffering from addiction and alcohol dependency and thinks that more money needs to be spent to repair the damage. Margaret thinks that investment in education is the key. Currently, education for First Nation children is underfunded by more than C$2,000 per student and only a few continue their studies. Most children live in families with parents and grandparents who never received higher education. She goes on to explain that one of the problems with the residential schools was that they were really educating the children for life as workers; sometimes they only spent half a day in school and the rest of the time learning how to farm or work in factories, the girls how to be domestic servants. As soon as they were fifteen they were forced to leave regardless of the grade they'd reached. There was no higher education for Native children. She gives a wry laugh as she adds,

"They weren't going to give them an education that might risk them growing up to be the equals of their oppressors."

As I turn off the light, I'm feeling very excited, but also really, really nervous about tomorrow. I've dreamed of this journey for so long it seems almost impossible that it will happen. And I'm also afraid that it won't live up to my expectations; it won't be what I've imagined, or that it won't give me what I'm looking for. Not that I even know what it is I am looking for. Something vague and hopelessly out of reach. That's what worries me, that I'll leave in two weeks time and still not know.

10. In Margaret Atwood's Bedroom

'…in this country they call Canada, there is another country called Haida Gwaii. To the people who live here, the Haida, theirs is not just another country; it is another culture, another cosmology, another reality, another economy, another history — another world.' [46]
Ian Gill, All That We Say is Ours

On Monday morning, early, I board a small turbo-prop Beechcraft at Vancouver South Terminal to fly to Masset at the north end of Haida Gwaii. It's a surprise to find that there's no security of the kind you get in England if you're boarding a domestic flight. I arrive at the airport and stroll out to the plane with some men in check shirts carrying a lot of fishing equipment. They are talking about the weather. Apparently it's very cloudy and they've heard that we might not be able to land at Masset, which is under a 'weather advisory'. There's also a small group, more smartly dressed, all wearing the Co-op logo, carrying briefcases and laptops and talking graphs and sales charts. Only one other woman.

I've forgotten how noisy turbo props are. As it bounces and shakes its way down the runway and into the air, the vibration and sound of the engines makes my ears hurt, but I've forgotten to bring ear plugs. The air stewardesses here have to have muscle. Before we took off, I watched a young, blonde girl hauling the boarding steps up into the aircraft and then folding them up like a gigantic buggy to slide into a recess in the fuselage. And I've learnt a new term for hand luggage; 'valet bags'. If the plane is full you have to put your valet bags on a trolley and the stewardess stuffs

them into any available gap at the front of the plane behind the
pilot.

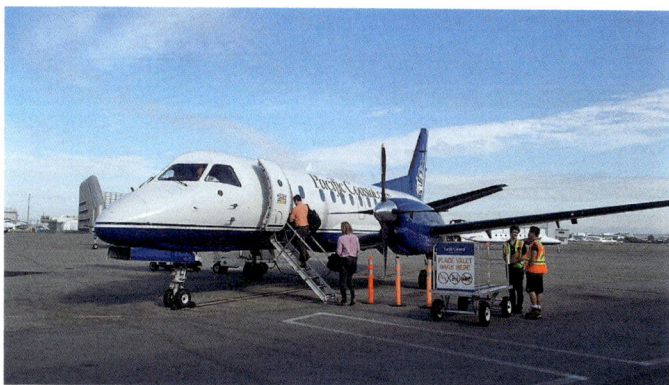

"Travelling by turboprop"

The flight goes over the coastal mountains. The rugged,
glaciated peaks that I could see from the streets of Vancouver are
still striped with snow. It takes over two hours to fly up to Masset
and the beautiful sunlight I'd been basking in at the airport
soon turns to cloud. The mountains disappear and all I can see
beneath me is a thick grey blanket and the shadow of the plane
racing across it. As we approach Masset and begin to descend, we
disappear into the cloud, only to re-emerge on our way back up
again. The pilot's voice crackles on the intercom as he tells us that
he can't see the runway, but will go around and try from another
direction. We make a second descent into the cloud, but again the
landing is aborted. The pilot says he's going to fly to Sandspit and
wait for better weather.

Sandspit is a small, ex-military, landing strip at the north
end of Moresby island, where a few people still live on the coast
around the airport. Moresby, the southern island, is otherwise
uninhabited, and contains Gwaii Haanas, a protected National
Park, part of it a World Heritage site. Unlike Masset, Sandspit
is clear and sunny. In the small airport, which looks rather like a
primary school without the children, a woman is making coffee

and sandwiches in the kitchen. She isn't quite ready, having expected to have only local customers as there weren't any flights due. But she heroically speeds up to satisfy a hungry group of stranded passengers.

On the TV screen at Sandspit, Perry Bellegarde, the Chief of all the First Nation people of Canada is talking about the 'Truth and Reconciliation' process. The final report by the Commission is due to be published tomorrow. Bellegarde refers to what he calls a 'cultural genocide' and he is very forthright about the attitudes of Canadians in general towards this period of their history. He says people still ask him, "Why don't you First Nation people just get on with it — why are you continually harping on about the past?" He says that his reply is always, "If you had suffered what we suffered, could you just get on with it?" Then he asks, "Do you say that to the Jews? Just get on with it? Never mind the holocaust?" He makes the point that they are still living with the consequences of three generations of broken families as well as broken communities and not enough investment for the future. What is needed, he says, echoing Margaret Atwood's words last night, is acknowledgement of what has been done and more money spent on education and housing to close the poverty gap.

It's an impassioned speech, both moving and eloquent. He ends by saying, "I urge everybody across Canada to rid themselves of things like the misconceptions about indigenous peoples, the discriminatory, racist attitudes that may exist, to move them out so that new things may come in. We do have a shared history, and we do have a shared responsibility going forward."[47]

We eat lunch and hang around for a couple of hours before getting the all clear to go back up to Masset. The pilot tells us he thinks he'll be able to land, but if not we'll be taken to Terrace, an airport on the mainland, across the Hecate Strait, one hundred and forty kilometres inland from the northernmost port of Prince Rupert. He doesn't say how we're to get from there to Masset. I'm seeing more of British Columbia than I'd planned. And I'm beginning to realise why flights here are so expensive.

Fortunately, this time we emerge from the cloud to a view of the ocean, a shoreline and a landscape carpeted by pine forest.

There are a few scattered buildings and a tarmac landing strip. A sharp bump and I am, finally, at my destination.

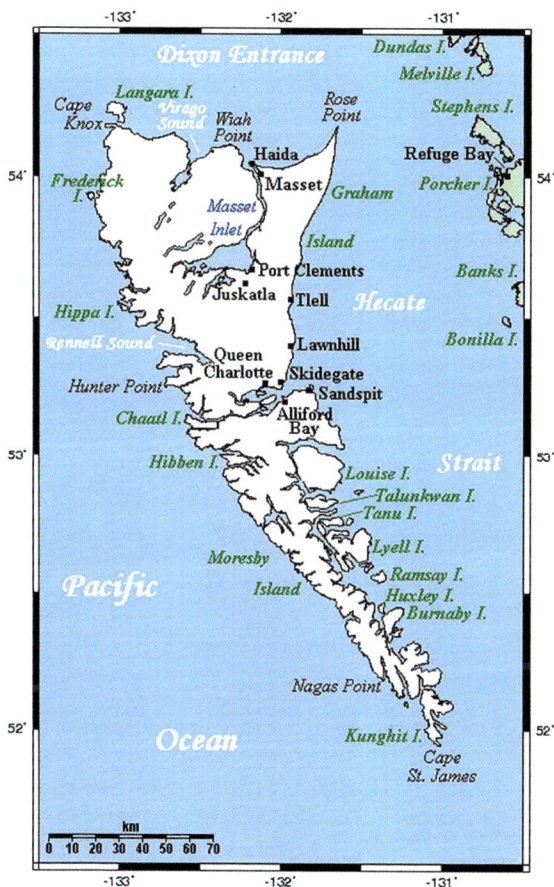

Haida Gwaii is composed of a number of islands, many of them very small. There are two main landmasses, Graham Island in the north and Moresby Island to the south. A thin strip of water separates them and their coastlines are a labyrinth of inlets and fjords containing smaller islands. After the smallpox epidemic of 1864, now referred to as 'The Great Dying', what was left of the Haida communities on Moresby Island were 'encouraged' by missionaries to move north onto Graham Island and combine with the remnants of other clans in 'Reserves' at two locations, Old Massett and Skidegate. For some historical analysts this amounted to ethnic cleansing, since it left the southern island free from its indigenous population and open for settlement and commercial exploitation, particularly logging and mining. It also separated many of the Haida people from the land that gave them their identity, their language, culture and livelihood. The Haida, like other First Nation people, believe that humanity is at one with the ecosystem they are part of. There is no separate thing called 'Nature'. When you look at it, this seems so obvious it shouldn't need explaining. So, to sever a people's links with their habitat is to cut them off from themselves. If, as one Australian aboriginal wrote, so powerfully, you can imagine one family continuously occupying the same land for thousands of years, 'using it not just to sustain life, but as a place of reverence and worship, where every tree, rock and water hole has significance, you will get some understanding of the importance of land to the Indigenous people.'[48]

For the Haida the move meant further disruption to their social structure; instead of living in distinct clan groups they had to merge with others in awkward combinations. There might be three chiefs in one small community. How could that possibly work? But somehow it had to be made to work. In Skidegate and Massett, bewildered families settled as best they could and got down to the business of feeding themselves and erecting houses to live in. The totems of their history and identity were left to rot on the seashore in front of houses that had now become mortuaries. A temporary evacuation became a permanent exile from their traditional homes. Haida Gwaii was re-christened the Queen Charlotte Islands and has only recently got its identity back.

In the nineteenth century, European immigrant communities were also becoming stabilised at Skidegate and Massett. The latter was an ideal location for fishing as well as a logging operation. New Masset (with only one T), as they called their settlement to distinguish it from the village on reserve land allocated to the Haida, was at the mouth of a deep water channel, Masset Sound, which goes more than thirty kilometres inland, like a deep, wide, saltwater river leading to a massive inland lake, Masset Inlet, where they established a logging station called Port Clements. Not only was New Masset inlet good for fishing and supply boats, it was also on the logging route, taking the timber from deep in the forest, through the processing depot at Port Clements, floating it out down Masset Sound at high tide and out to the open ocean.

Today Masset doesn't have a ferry, but it does have Graham Island's only airport connecting with Vancouver, which is why I've travelled to Masset first. Choosing somewhere to stay was tricky at a distance. There isn't a lot of tourist accommodation on Haida Gwaii, so I had to do some careful research online. There are plenty of log cabin type self-catering units but, travelling on my own and without a car, I need to be more central, to be near all the things I want to see. And I want the opportunity to meet people, to talk to them about Haida Gwaii. Solitude is fine when you choose it, but you also need to be able to choose to be sociable sometimes.

The B&B that caught my eye was one called Copper Beech, which had stunning reviews on Trip Advisor. It was owned until recently by an eccentric hippy who was also an antique dealer and given to throwing impromptu parties. His name was David Phillips, a man who came to the island as a young, wealthy adventurer who had originally intended to go to China. He jumped ship in Prince Rupert, came across to Masset out of curiosity, and bought an old sailing boat which he immediately wrecked on the treacherous coast. Like many others, he 'washed up' at Copper Beech and never left.

The house has a similarly peripatetic history. It was originally built by a Swedish carpenter for a fish cannery manager at George Point — quite a distance along the coast from Masset. When it changed hands in 1921 it was floated on logs down Masset Sound to the Watun River, where it stayed for eleven years before being towed to the government docks in New Masset and winched up on the shoreline of the fishing harbour among the boatsheds and other old properties that line the water's edge. It got its name from the copper beech tree planted outside by a nostalgic English bride.

In Margaret Atwood's Bedroom

When David Phillips arrived it was owned by a Masset character called Sidney Smith who ran it as a 'dollar-a-night flop house'. David became a permanent resident, first as a tenant, then as owner, caring for Sidney when he became an invalid and repairing and altering the fabric of the building. Everyone stayed with him when they came to Haida Gwaii, including former President Trudeau and his wife. David appears in photographs as a commanding figure in a caftan, brandishing a wine glass. His generosity and his cooking were legendary. Although not a First Nation man himself, David had many friends among the Haida people of Old Massett and his house was, as they remember, the place where 'much of Masset's narrative flowed'[49] for more than thirty years.

Since David died Copper Beech has been owned by Susan Musgrave, who also came to Masset in the nineteen seventies. The name gave me quite a jolt. Musgrave is a common name in the part of Cumbria where I live. There are two small villages called Little Musgrave and Great Musgrave. The Musgraves were, until the 19th century, one of the great warring clans known as the Border Reivers. The lands between England and Scotland had been fought over for centuries (the Roman Emperor Hadrian built a wall) and even after the Scots had finally been defeated in the 14th century, the area was lawless, held by powerful families whose feuds and raids on each other's property led to it becoming known as The Debatable Lands. Farms were pillaged and burnt, men slaughtered, cattle, horses, sheep and women abducted, land boundaries established by deeds of the illegal variety. The Musgraves were among the most successful of the robber barons. Like a present day mafia, people paid them to be left alone. They inspired Sir Walter Scott's ballads 'The Minstrelsy of the Scottish Border' and a host of local legends. At some point in the 17th century, under James the First, the warring clans became respectable. Since then, many clan members have emigrated and it seems that at least one branch of the family went to British Columbia.

One of my Facebook friends, a Canadian writer called Barbara Lambert, contacted me as soon as she heard where I was going

108

and said, "You must get in contact with Susan Musgrave. She's a writer and a good poet. It would be nice for you to meet up." So I took Barbara's advice and booked at Copper Beech, sending Susan an email. We 'friended' each other on Facebook, as you do these days. I thought it would be wonderful to meet another writer, particularly a poet, living on Haida Gwaii. Then I discovered that Susan is indeed one of the local Musgraves. Her ruined ancestral home, Eden Hall, is only a few miles from where I live. She has a photograph of herself, taken between the imposing gateposts, which is all that is left of the house.

On the internet, the airport seemed to be just a short distance from town so I'd anticipated being able to walk, or that there would be taxis or some kind of shuttle. But I hadn't realised that it would be so small — just an airstrip. Outside there's only a car park and my fellow passengers are either being met or have vehicles parked there and I'm no longer sure whether the distance is walkable with luggage. I go inside and ask the woman at the flight desk, who is just packing up to go home. She telephones for a taxi to come out for me and I wait, the last person on the kerb, feeling rather lost.

Haida Time, when it comes, isn't just a taxi service, it's a complete tour. The female driver is welcoming and incredibly kind. As we drive into town she points out all the different roads, the houses, the little shops, where I can hire a car if I want one and tells me where to find a meal, "They all close early here, so be sure to get in there before they do." Then she tells me about local coffee shops and where to buy souvenirs. There's no need for a tourist information service, which is apparently still closed for the winter; my driver tells me everything I need to know about Masset.

Copper Beech doesn't disappoint. The wooden house, painted in red and blue, looks small under the umbrella of beech leaves, but inside it opens out, on three levels, like a tardis. The deck outside is spread with rugs and chairs with a random assortment of cushions and blankets. I'd been warned in advance that Susan was away doing a poetry reading in Toronto, so I'm met by Elle, who has just arrived to take care of the house for the summer. She is warm and welcoming even though she is about to go out. Apparently the washing machine has broken down, irreparably, and someone is going to take her to see a woman who can do the laundry. I'm immediately aware of the negative side of living so far off the beaten track. A new washing machine will have to be ordered from the mainland, trucked onto a ferry and then driven the length of Graham Island before it can be installed. That's several days at least, and there are no launderettes on Haida Gwaii.

Elle shows me my room before she dashes out. I'm staying in the Chadwick Room — the only one that was available when I booked. It's named for an adventurous, but mysterious, woman called Florence Chadwick. Apparently David Phillips, when he was an antique dealer, acquired a steamer trunk full of her possessions, including passport. Who was she and what happened to her? No one seems to know, but some of her memorabilia decorates the room, which has a wonderful view of the garden. It's a bit like moving into an antique shop — not one of the items is standard issue for a hotel room, but everything has a glorious serendipity. I unpack and creep down the back stairs to my little shower cubicle in the basement, before picking up a book from Mrs Chadwick's bookshelf and going outside to soak up the sun on the deck. I make a cup of tea in the kitchen and take a piece of the carrot cake on the dining room table beside a label that says 'please help yourself'. I expect to change shape at any moment, like Alice in Wonderland.

Other residents begin to arrive. Two women, of a similar age to myself, wheel their bicycles through the gate. They have cycled all the way from a small community in northern British Columbia, via Prince Rupert, the ferry to Skidegate and ninety five kilometres of road north to Masset. I admire their leg muscles and their fitness. They make me feel pale and indoorsy. Both women are church volunteers with First Nation youth organisations at summer camps. One of them tells a story that makes me feel very uncomfortable. After church one day, she had been followed and threatened by a man with a knife. When questioned he said that he thought she had been laughing at him, because she had made a comment about his new glasses. She excused him because he'd been through hell in a residential school where he'd been abused, and then he'd had drug problems and mental health issues. "But I was sad," she adds, "After all we've done for him." When I analyse my reaction later, I realise that the discomfort came from the feeling that there was a slightly patronising note in her voice, and no understanding that the man's anger might be directed against her as a representative of the very Christian organisation that had abused him.

I'm in my room, beginning to sort out my computer and my notebooks, when I hear a male voice in the sitting room talking to Elle. He and his girlfriend are booked into the room next to mine, The Retreat, but he's more than six feet tall and the bed is on the small side. It's a problem. Elle would like to swap them, but the house is full. I put my head out of the door and offer them my queen-size bed. I haven't yet used the bed or the towels, so it would be simple to relocate my possessions next door. And that's how I meet Bill and Katie.

They have walked and hitchhiked back to Masset, after camping up in the nature reserve near North Beach, and they are damp, tired and aching, both in need of a hot shower and a comfortable bed. Bill tells me he's a doctor, from a small town to the north of Vancouver. He's having trouble with his back, after sleeping on hard ground, and very grateful for the offer of a swap.

I can't believe my luck, as I move my luggage and my clothes into The Retreat. It had been my original first choice, but because it was already booked I'd had to take the Chadwick room. The Retreat is carpentered like a ship's cabin, with a bed fitted across the end wall. There's a big window at the foot of the bed that looks straight out onto the harbour with the fishing boats bobbing around on the tide. The beech tree drapes its branches down like a blind. There's a writing desk under the window with a small chair. The curtains are peacock blue silk embroidered with gold motifs and on the chest of drawers beside the bed there's a huge bowl filled with shells and pebbles, feathers and bones, even a

Margaret Atwood's bedroom at Copper Beech

meteorite — a treasure trove of beach-combing. It's a room full
of stories and I love it. The only disadvantage is that you have
to walk through the communal sitting room and kitchen to
the bathroom, but it's worth the inconvenience. The bathroom
is as quirky as the rest of the house — a claw footed bath and
assorted fitments, none of which quite match, but are somehow
more special than any pristine hotel facilities.

The one thing that brings me up short is the notice on the
bedroom wall. 'What to do in case of Earthquakes'. Haida Gwaii
is on the shifting plate of the Pacific Rim and seismic tremors are
a regular feature. Occasionally there are mega-quakes. Only two
years ago there was a 7.7 that rattled everything very thoroughly.
Sometimes, historically, there are tsunamis. The instructions ask
all the guests, in the event of a warning, to assemble outside to be
transported to the high 'safe point' designated by the government.
It brings back horrible memories of driving through dark streets,
around the rubble of collapsed buildings, up broken roads,
avoiding landslides to safe ground in New Zealand, after a big
quake, until the all-clear was given. I hope that nothing like that

happens while I'm in Masset. The world doesn't get much wilder than an earthquake of more than 7 on the Richter Scale.

I share a cup of tea with the doctor's girlfriend. Katie turns out to be a writer too. She's just published a novel called *The Bears*, about the plight of the wild animals caught up in the environmental mess that is the Alberta tar sands and its associated transportation hazards. In the novel, a pipeline begins to leak, endangering the wild bears. A group of environmental scientists and First Nation people fight to save their shared landscape. Katie was once a tree planter, replanting the areas that had been logged out. She is a passionate environmentalist and fascinated by First Nation, particularly Haida, culture. "We came here because of *The Bears*," she tells me. Bill and Katie are getting married soon and have come to Haida Gwaii to have their wedding rings made by a Haida jeweller. They show me the beautiful, carved rings which they're wearing for safe keeping until they get home.

They've just come back from a two day trip to Rose Spit, camping overnight. I feel quite depressed to discover that you can't do it one day, walking, as I'd planned to do. The beach is a twenty two kilometre walk each way, not including the distance from Masset to North Beach, and quite difficult underfoot. I realise that, beyond looking at photographs and maps on the internet, I haven't really done enough research into the practicality of the places I desperately want to get to. As I watch Bill and Katie shaking the sand out of the sleeping bags and pegging the tent to the washing line, I realise I haven't got the right equipment either. But, they tell me sternly, going alone isn't an option here for someone like me (presumably female and 'of a certain age'). There's no mobile phone signal, it's rough physical terrain, and there are bears in the woods.

In the warm afternoon sunshine I begin to explore Masset. At the end of the street the road turns right over the bridge that crosses the inlet, now an expanse of mud at low tide, to join the main road to the south of Graham Island. In the other direction are the two or three streets that form New Masset and the road that follows the coast towards Old Massett. I walk down to where I've been told there are shops and cafés, between rows of wooden villas set in well-kept gardens with flowerbeds and lawns. Almost every house has a blue 'No Enbridge' sign outside, opposing the Northern Gateway pipeline project. I pass one of the white, steepled churches that Emily Carr painted, and a big high-school building surrounded by grass. There's a gas station, which also seems to be a garage, and a booze shop selling every kind of imported wine and beer. The café that serves Chinese and Canadian food is shut, though I'm assured it will open for the summer season; another Chinese café is also closed, with a sign offering it for sale for C$100,000. The Green Café — that was recommended to me is also shut, but might be open tomorrow. I walk past the job centre, which has groups of men standing outside smoking, and there's a bank, but — as I'd been warned — it doesn't take any of my cards. The money I've got in my pocket will have to last for the whole of my stay here.

Next I tackle the shopping, looking for picnic food for packed lunches and economical evening meals. When I go into the Co-op supermarket I get a shock. It's as big as anything back home in England and it has a lot more stock. It wouldn't be out of place in London. You can buy anything here, from Italian Prosciutto and German Wurst, to mangoes and Camembert, hummous and gourmet yogurt. The prices reflect the fact that it's all been trucked, or air-freighted, thousands of miles to get here. When I think that the Haida fed themselves very well on the food that was available in the environment for free — salmon, crabs, halibut, clams, herring roe, venison, eggs, duck, goose, whale and seal meat, sea weed, cranberries, salmon-berries, mushrooms and a host of other delicacies — I wonder why it's necessary for this expensive, much-travelled food to be here. There's a whole aisle of bottled water, even though the tap water on the island is perfectly drinkable. I was asked, in advance, to bring my own re-usable water bottle with me, because the litter of plastic bottles that washes up from the Pacific Ocean on the coast of Haida Gwaii is such a problem. There are no recycling facilities here.

I buy bread and soup, cold meat, cheese and fruit. The final bill makes my eyes open very wide indeed.

Opposite the supermarket, there's a European-style coffee shop that appears to be thriving. I have a mug of dark Canadian coffee that sets every nerve cell buzzing with its caffeine kick. The walls are hung with the work of local artists. I could be almost anywhere in the world as I sit here in a comfortable armchair with my coffee on the carved wooden table in front of me. From the conversations, I gather that they're expecting a delivery of furniture from Ikea at any moment and my heart sinks. On the counter is a big warning about the effects of radiation from Fukishima which they are worried could turn up on the beaches here to ruin their fisheries. Everything, the Haida say, is connected, and so I shouldn't be surprised that even these remote islands have been touched by the tentacles of Big Commerce and Global Pollution. But I do get a sense that this is a community with a very vibrant environmental conscience, struggling with the demands of 'incomers' and tourists who expect international standards.

Walking back along the shoreline of the inlet, there are boat sheds and workshops. Eagles wheel overhead looking for food. There are no totem poles here and no Bighouses. This is European Masset and almost everyone I've met or who has served me has been European. Where, I wonder, are the Haida? Apart from my taxi driver, I haven't met any yet, though I know that several very high profile members of the Haida Nation were brought up here.

One of them, whose history is firmly rooted in Masset, is Haida artist and political activist Guujaaw, a former President of the Haida Nation. He was born Gary Edenshaw in 1953, one of nine children, inheriting his clan from his mother, who was a Raven from Skedans. Gary grew up in the European settlement of New Masset, which meant that he avoided being sent to the residential school in Alert Bay. His name change isn't uncommon. The Haida are often given new names at important points in their lives. Gary Edenshaw soon became Giindajin, which means 'full of questions' because of his restless, enquiring nature, and, as a young adult, rapidly becoming the spokesperson for his community, he was given Guujaaw, which means 'Drum', but also has the sense of 'voice', and that is the name he is now known by.

Guujaaw became interested in music as a teenager — drumming, playing the guitar, dancing, learning all the old Haida traditional songs he could find, listening to the Elders. He and his wife lived up at North Beach on an abandoned claim lot, at a place called Chicken Shit Harry's. There Guujaaw gradually made the transition from musician to master carver and then to political activist. The young Haida artists Gwaii and Jaalen Edenshaw are his sons and I'm quite likely to bump into them around here too.

After the second world war a military base was built in Masset and this created some tension in the local community. In the nineteen seventies, the two Massets apparently 'had a reputation as a tough town'. The area was a destination for 'hippies and draft dodgers', creating a very mixed community. Not surprisingly, the first significant stirring of Haida resistance occurred here, when an act of civil disobedience destroyed the lighthouse at Old Massett. This had been erected as part of a deal with the Band Council. It could be built on Haida land in exchange for money to fund improvements to their reserve. The lighthouse was built but the money never materialised, so the Haida took it down. Later,

Guujaaw and his friend and fellow activist, Michael Yahgulanaas, put the lighthouse beacon on a cedar pole and raised it in Massett as a trophy.

Guujaaw would go on to work with Bill Reid, particularly on Raven and the First Men, but politics were beginning to overtake art. As his political conscience grew he became involved in a number of environmental confrontations over logging concessions on Haida Gwaii. As a result of the movement he helped to create, the national park of Gwaii Hanaas was established on Moresby Island, preserving some of the most important ancient forest in British Columbia, and the abandoned Haida village of Ninstints, with its unique totem poles, became a World Heritage site. Guujaaw was subsequently elected as President of the Council of the Haida Nation in 2000, a position he held for twelve years, and he is still a prominent figure in the Haida campaign to have their land rights restored. The legal case of *The Council of the Haida Nation and Guujaaw V Her Majesty the Queen, the Province of British Columbia and Attorney General of Canada*, is as yet unresolved.

In the last two decades, the First Nation people have come to the forefront of the environmental movement all over North America. In the coffee shop I picked up the local paper, the *Haida Gwaii Observer*, and read an article about Greenpeace increasingly working with First Nation people to protect the environment. Greenpeace originated in Vancouver, so I suppose I shouldn't have been surprised. But I hadn't known that when the Greenpeace vessel Esperanza sailed into icy northern waters to oppose Shell's arctic drilling operation, representatives of six different Canadian First Nations were part of the crew. This activism has apparently grown out of land preservation movements headed by Guujaaw and his fellow activists. The piece was written by Ralph Stocker, an Old Massett resident who has also featured in a number of Haida documentary films. In the article he refers to the anti-logging protest led by Guujaaw in the nineteen eighties and its importance for the Haida community. 'Re-awakenings happened. We were reminded of our responsibilities to the land, sea and air — to respect our ancestors and ourselves.'[50]

Back at Copper Beech I make soup and sandwiches and eat them on the terrace with Elle. Bill and Katie are out and the two women from the north have gone to the diner for a burger and chips. Elle tells me that it's her first time on Haida Gwaii. She came just as Susan left, so has been pitched into the deep end. But she already loves it. The air smells of salt and pine resin and there's going to be a full moon tonight. We talk companionably, wrapped in blankets against the evening chill, until the sun has set and all the travelling begins to catch up with me. I head for The Retreat and tuck myself into my bunk, looking out over the inlet and the bobbing masts of the boats. I read for a while, until I hear the other residents return, all goodnights have been said and doors closed. People go to bed early here.

As I lie in the late twilight, I can hear the house settling all around me — the two bicycling ladies have run a thundering bath above my head, the doctor is snoring creatively next door beside his girlfriend, both wearing their new Haida wedding rings. While underneath, a middle aged, middle class couple — last minute arrivals — are keeping themselves to themselves. Elle has taken her pillow and her mug of tea to whatever bivouac she has across the garden. The light is fading out of the sky and the sea fog has drifted in and swallowed the moon. The sea eagles are still shrieking at each other in the harbour, which is just below my feet, through the window at the bottom of my bed.

This was Margaret Atwood's bedroom when she stayed here. She could have had any of the expensive, en suite, rooms upstairs or downstairs, but she chose this one. It was, she tweeted 'unique, luverly'. What's good enough for Margaret Atwood is good enough for me.

11. Two Massets

*'It is one of the world's greatest tributes to the strength of the
human spirit that most of those who lived, and their
children after them, remained sane and adapted.'*
Bill Reid

I wake up to the smell of coffee. It's breakfast time. Elle has the
table set with home-baked bread (Susan is famous for her soda
bread), homemade jams and marmalades, thick white yogurt and
a mixed fruit crumble made from berries gathered in the wild.
There are fresh, young, spruce tips sprinkled in the yogurt — a
new taste for me, and they have a kind of citrus zest. Elle explains
that you can make tea with them, which is very good for coughs
and colds. You can also mix them with mayonnaise to make a
sauce for salmon.

We eat our breakfast from an assortment of antique bowls
and plates with ornate silver spoons and the kind of knives my
grandmother kept in the Sunday drawer. As I spoon up my fruit
crumble and yogurt, I keep thinking about all the wild food in
England that we let go to waste — the wild blackberries and crab
apples that rot on the branches of our woodlands while we buy
preserves in jars from the supermarket; the spring glut of elder
flower in the hedges that doesn't get a second glance, while sales
of elder flower cordial in green bottles double every year. Most
of us don't even know what we could eat from the fields and
hedgerows; that plant knowledge has long gone and only a few
people still have it. Foraging, except in Tesco or Sainsbury's, isn't
something we do any more.

It's a day of departures at Copper Beech. The two adventurous women on bicycles have their saddle-bags loaded up ready for the road south towards the ferry. Bill and Katie are also departing for Skidegate. Katie signs a copy of her novel and leaves it on the shelf in the sitting room, alongside the work of other occupants, past and present. I feel guilty that, keeping the weight of my luggage within limits for the small planes I have to travel on, I haven't brought any of my own books with me. We exchange addresses and websites. This is a house for kindred spirits.

Today I'm intending to shake off the inertia of two days of travel and go for a long walk in the Delkatla Nature Reserve which begins at the end of the street. The salt-water inlet seeps into the woods at high tide and there are small lakes and marshes that attract birds and other wildlife. So, with a packed rucksack and a bottle of water, I set off for the woods without a map.

My mother had a saying, from a piece she'd cut out of the *Woman's Weekly* in the nineteen fifties; 'Go to the woods in company and you come back empty: go alone and you come home with more than you can hold'. As a teenager I used to laugh at her homely quotations and platitudes cut out of magazines. But that one is true. Solitude is hard to find and we need it. Contemporary life is stressful. We move quickly from place to place, we interact with a lot of people in the process, and we are constantly bombarded with information. Our senses are frayed by the overload.

I have arrived on this remote island bringing the twenty-first century with me. I have a Kindle Fire with an entire library of books on it; my laptop so that I can work; and I have a smart phone with all my ferry, plane and accommodation bookings on it as well as a map of what time it is anywhere in the world. I can take a photograph and fire it up to a satellite into the full view of everyone who knows me, and a lot of others who don't, in a few seconds. There is no such thing as a private experience in this modern age. I regret that. But stepping back from social media is difficult — your children, your partner, your friends, are somehow affronted if you don't want to talk to them or be available all the time. Because it's possible it's expected of us.

So, hiding in the woods beyond the reach of mobile phone signals, news bulletins, Twitter and any kind of human contact feels very good even if it's only for a few hours. I've always had this need for solitude. Ever since I was a child, for a short part of every day, I've had to close the door, rather selfishly, and just Be On My Own. I call it Creative Space and it seems to be something that a lot of other human beings need too; a small absence when you can hear your own thoughts, your heartbeat, a little pause in the music. Andrew Marvell, in his hymn to a garden paradise called it 'a green thought in a green shade'.

A few months before I left I read *The Book of Silence*, by Sara Maitland, an autobiographical essay on how, although otherwise compulsively sociable and addicted to words, she increasingly sought to live alone in isolated places in complete silence. My problem with the book was that although she used the word solitude interchangeably with silence, she never distinguished the words from each other. They are not the same. Solitude doesn't necessarily require silence. Mine is usually full of chatter — reading a book, listening to music, here and now listening to the polyphony of noises in the forest around me. Solitude for me is freedom from the need to interact with other human beings, a time when nothing is required of me. My heart rate slows, the blood stops thudding in my ears, the mind wanders off on pathways of its own. Sometimes words start to write themselves and demand to be written down. May Sarton, in her *Journal of a Solitude*, wrote that it was 'Cracking open the inner world again', which was both restorative and dangerous because there was 'nothing to cushion against attacks from within'.[51] You can find yourself facing your very own D'Sonoqua.

These are young woods, second growth, but very pretty, and you can hear the trees breathing as the constant wind blows over them from the direction of the ocean. The morning mists are beginning to clear and I can see the daily flight from Vancouver, dropping down towards the airstrip, arriving on time today. The vegetation under the trees is lush. There's normally a lot of rainfall here; as much as two hundred inches a year on the Pacific-facing coast, but it hasn't rained for a month now. The temperatures are still very high and I haven't needed to put on my fleece mountain jacket once since I've been in Canada. The internet news bulletin I looked at this morning, before I came out, blames it onto the behaviour of the Jet Stream, which has become blocked off the west coast and is causing 'an unusual doldrum'. "Weather patterns," the meteorologist said, "just aren't supposed to last this long."[52] On the mainland, lakes are drying up and snow has melted from the Rockies unusually fast. 2014 was a record-breaking year in British Columbia and it looks as if 2015 is going to be another.

I'm not alone in becoming convinced that what we are creating on this planet is wilder and more dangerous than our weirdest imaginings. Scientists all over the world, conservationists, economists, some politicians, even the Pope, are raising their voices to warn us of the consequences if we don't change the way we live. According to a recent report by the World Wildlife Fund, 50% of all wildlife species on the planet have disappeared in the last forty years. The report points out the insanity of our pattern of consumption. 'Currently, the global population is cutting down trees faster than they regrow, catching fish faster than the oceans can restock, pumping water from rivers and aquifers faster than rainfall can replenish them and emitting more climate-warming carbon dioxide than oceans and forests can absorb.'[53] We have already altered the natural balance that created a nurturing environment for us all, and we are now in the grip of something savage and untameable. The Wild has us firmly in its claws. The future is uncertain and frightening.

A friend has suggested that many of us are suffering from a new phenomenon, becoming common among scientists and writers and environmental activists. Its milder symptoms are, 'stress, anxiety, and depression, an inexplicable feeling of sadness, a sense of hopelessness, fatalism, resignation'. At the more extreme end, people are reporting 'strains on social relationships, substance abuse, loss of autonomy and sense of control'. Those who are confronting climate change and environmental destruction on a daily basis are being overwhelmed by their fears and their sense of loss. They are, literally, grieving for the world we are losing. But it goes unacknowledged. 'The notion that our individual grief and emotional loss can actually be a reaction to the decline of our air, water, and ecology rarely appears in conversation or the media.'[54]

Sand Cranes, Masset

The sea is beginning to creep into the marshland as I walk. The ground under my feet is cracked and dry. I'm following the footprints of the wild cattle that live here, once owned by settlers, but now feral. On my right two sand cranes are grazing the marsh. They look up as I pass, but don't seem alarmed. I eat my lunch on a rickety wooden landing stage at an inland lake. A pair of aggressive squirrels come down from the trees and chatter at me in an agitated way, as if telling me I shouldn't be here. They're about the same size as the red squirrels back home in the Lake District, but a much darker colour. These squirrels were introduced to the islands in 1947 by foresters to make fir cone collection easier. The plan was that the squirrels would do it for them and the tree planters would just raid the squirrels' caches. It didn't work well, but the squirrels have thrived and are now a pest, threatening native species of birds by stealing their eggs.

But in spite of the squirrels' predation, there are birds everywhere here, wading, flying and floating. The animals are more elusive, though I do glimpse a deer in the dappled shade on the other side of the water. It is a very peaceful place, but it's parkland, reclaimed from domestic use, being 're-wilded'. I can't help but think that observing animals in 'the wild' in a sanctuary with curated viewings is really only an outdoor zoo.

I'm still puzzling out the definitions of the word 'wild'. It's one of the most over-used words in the dictionary and means so many different things to different people. Perhaps Robert Bringhurst has the most simple definition; 'it means undomesticated, unmanaged, uncontrolled by human beings'. He adds that 'it disappears from view wherever an industry arises. And that includes the tourist industry'.[55] So there's no point in complaining about being in a curated landscape. I am part of the problem of the disappearing wilderness.

I come out of the woods in the centre of Masset and, after another bracing mug of coffee in the café, make my way down onto the coast road towards that other Massett, where the indigenous population originally built their Bighouses and which then became a kind of refugee community for the survivors of other villages decimated by disease. There were (and still are) two Massets; New Masset, 'a municipality under Canadian legislation' and the original village of Old Massett, on 'reserved land', 'under the Constitution of the Haida Nation'. This separation between settlers and indigenous people was, in the words of one commentator, 'fairly consistent with the Canadian approach, which [was] to stick all the Indians in one place and provide all the commercial services right outside, so they are basically a market pool for the corner store'.[56] Under the strict terms of the Indian Act non-Indians couldn't enter reserve land without permission, so it's not surprising that businesses were set up outside in areas controlled by Europeans. Again, under the terms of the Indian Act, these businesses could not be owned by indigenous people. As perpetual children they couldn't own anything. They were not there to become independent entrepreneurs, they were there to serve and consume. That policy is at the root of many First Nation problems today.

Old Massett is three and a half miles along the coast towards the mouth of the Inlet. The British named it Dixon's Entrance, after the sea captain who arrived in 1787. Almost a hundred years later, a Haida chief described the arrival of the Europeans, as it had been told to him. 'A very long time ago,' he said, 'a ship under sail appeared in the vicinity of North Island. The Indians were all very much afraid. The chief shaked in the general fear, but feeling that it was necessary for the sake of his dignity to act a bold part, he dressed himself in all the finery worn in dancing, went out to sea in his canoe, and on approaching the ship performed a dance.'[57] Their fear was justified. Captain George Dixon appropriated the islands for the Crown and re-named them the Queen Charlotte Islands, the name of his ship and the monarch's wife.

The tide is swilling in as I walk, almost full, smelling strongly of kelp. It runs very fast. I'm thinking about another woman, Florence Edenshaw, walking this same path along the coast, over a hundred years ago, with her husband-to-be Robert Davidson. Florence was the middle daughter of Charles Edenshaw, one of the most important Haida carvers of all time, a great artist and hereditary chief who lived in Old Massett. Florence told her story to researcher Margaret Blackman in 1982. In December 1910, Florence had just had her fourteenth birthday and her marriage was imminent. Robert was bringing her to New Masset to buy her presents, just before Christmas. 'He told me I could buy anything I wanted.' There was snow on the ground and she walked fast, keeping as far away as she could, 'so I don't go close to him'.

Robert Davidson was Haida royalty, a hereditary chief from an important family, but he was much older than Florence (nearly thirty) and had been married before to a woman who had died of TB. Florence Edenshaw, although she wasn't aware of it, was of similar rank, being the daughter of a great chief. The marriage had been arranged by Robert's relatives and by Florence's uncle, according to custom. She told her parents that she would run away if they made her marry him. But two months after that winter walk on the beach she was married in the church at Massett. 'I was stubborn; I wouldn't say the promises. I guess I thought I wouldn't be really married if I didn't answer when they asked me. I felt bad the whole time.' Even as an old woman the memory of the wedding was one she didn't want to revisit. 'Everybody but me was real happy. I don't remember any more about the wedding, it was too awful.'[58]

Charles Edenshaw

It's important not to sentimentalise the Haida. Before the Europeans arrived, they were a formidable people, dominating other First Nation tribes along the north west coast, famous for their prowess in war, and for the heads they took back to their villages as trophies. Charles Edenshaw himself remembered having taken part in just such a raid when he was a young man. They also seized and kept slaves, who did much of the menial work for the clan. Many of their practices now seem barbaric to us, though common in other cultures. One of these is the practice of arranging marriages for their children. The Haida usually made these arrangements when their children reached puberty, but the outcome was often unhappy. Florence was pressured into just such a marriage in 1911, though she was a remarkable woman and eventually made a success of the relationship. She was lucky to be married to a man who appears to have been extremely considerate. Although at first Florence refused to consummate the marriage, she and her husband Robert eventually had thirteen children. Two of them died in the residential schools; her son Arnold fell from a ladder while painting the school wall and a daughter, Helen, died in an epidemic. Three other children died from accident or illness. Seven members of her remaining family still live in the two Masset communities and her grandson, also called Robert Davidson, is now one of the most famous artists in North America.

My legs are beginning to ache when the first totem pole comes into view. It's of modest height, only a little higher than the electricity pole in front of it and looks rather out of place on the edge of the street with an ordinary suburban house behind it. But that's how things are these days. It's very exciting to see any modern totem poles at all. In a photograph taken around 1879, fifteen years before Florence Davidson was born, this whole bay was lined with Bighouses, fronted by totem poles and mortuary poles, a whole forest of them, some three or four times the height of the houses. In front of them, along the shoreline, where the road is now, was an expanse of eelgrass going down to the sand, with boats and canoes pulled up on the beach. It all looks very different today.

There are two streets in Old Massett, named for Eagle and Raven. Raven Road is the one facing the sea, and there's a line of ravens keeping watch on the wall that separates the tarmac from the beach. The buildings are an odd mixture of tidy suburban dwellings and houses that look quite derelict, with patched roofs and broken windows, gardens filled with discarded objects, burnt out cars. The poverty shocks me. It is so very different to its twin three miles down the road. In one there is, not exactly affluence, but an atmosphere of quiet self-sufficiency. Here there is an obvious need. In New Masset there's a tourist trade; here, none that I can find. I've been told that there's a café and I'd really like to try it. I'm desperate for a drink and some calories before tackling the walk back to Copper Beech, but I can't find anything.

Either I'm not looking in the right place, or it's closed for winter. My legs are too tired to explore any further and so I turn round to walk back in a melancholy mood.

Neglected house, Old Massett

Various people I've talked to since I came to British Columbia have told me that the young First Nation people apparently feel inadequate and discouraged from any kind of aspiration. Their traditional way of life has gone and not been replaced by anything. Pride and self-esteem have been destroyed. In many cases, the vacuum has been filled by depression, alcoholism and drug addiction. Underlying it is a feeling of anger (why wouldn't there be?). The Indian Act has never been repealed and, although indigenous people were finally allowed to vote in 1960, they are still treated as second-class citizens. There is 80% unemployment among the young Haida here. Marika Wilbur, a Native American photographer, who has made it her life's work to photograph every First Nation tribe on the continent, posed an important question; 'What happens when a people have lost their connection to the land, to their spirit, and to the things that make them whole?' The answer was a tragic reality: 'they turn to things that fill those holes inside of them … things like drugs and alcohol'.[59] I should be looking at a strong Haida community in charge of their own island, their own destiny. What I feel is enormous sadness.

This lack of confidence, the absence of aspiration, is also obvious in Florence Edenshaw Davidson's memoir. She was a high status Haida woman and an artist in her own right, respected and honoured in her own community, the wife of a chief, and yet she never felt good enough. When she and her husband were asked to go to Victoria to launch and name a new barge, she felt unworthy and said that people wouldn't go to the event because 'we're just Indians'. In 1971 she was presented to the Queen.

This is a particular problem for First Nation women, who had their own independent status before the Europeans arrived. It was, and still is, a matrilineal society. The next chief was never the son of the current chief, but the son of the chief's eldest sister. Women could also be chiefs, or shamans, and — in contrast to the second-class status of European women — they had their own valued role in tribal life, passing on their songs, stories and clan knowledge. A man took his moiety and his clan status from his mother. A Raven mother married to an Eagle father would have only Raven children, and she kept her own name. But when the Europeans arrived they enforced the values of patriarchal society on all First Nation women. Legally, everything was now passed down the male line. They had to take their husband's name on marriage, which was so preposterous that one First Nation woman famously asked in disbelief, "How can a Raven woman have an Eagle name?" It is the reason that many women keep their own names, as well as adding their husband's, when they marry, as Florence Edenshaw Davidson did. One other consequence of patriarchal values, was that a woman could only take her status from her husband, so that a First Nation woman marrying a European man, lost her right to her 'Indian' ethnicity in the eyes of the state.

On the sea front, at the edge of the pavement, is a memorial to the man who adopted Florence's mother, orphaned in the smallpox epidemic. His 'Christian' name was Albert Edward Edenshaw, and he was a very important figure in Haida society. His life bridged the before and after of colonisation. As a great chief he owned houses in several locations including Old Massett, kept slaves and had two wives. In 1834 he built the house he had first seen in a dream at Kiusta — a village on the coast just north west of Old Massett. This building was the famous Myth House, sometimes called the House of Stories, which his nephew and heir Charles Edenshaw (Florence's father) later reproduced as a model, and which is now in a museum in New York. Its facade illustrated the 'Lazy Son-in-Law' story, where a young man, whose mother-in-law constantly accuses him of laziness, tricks her into believing she is a shaman by catching fish and whales during the night and laying them at her door. She boasts about her abilities and then dies of shame when she finds out that it is her son-in-law who is actually the shaman. Charles Edenshaw should have succeeded his uncle as Chief at Kiusta, but the 'Great Dying' intervened and both Albert Edward and Charles eventually made their homes in Massett.

Corvid

While I'm reading the inscription and taking a photograph, one of the Elders walks past me and stops to chat. She asks me what I'm doing here and I explain, haltingly, that I'm a writer and want to write about my experiences. I also tell her about the poems I'm working on. Her response isn't one I'd anticipated.

"Do you have permission?" she asks.

"Do I need permission?"

"If you're writing about us, you do!" She tells me that I will have to talk to the Band Council. The office is closed at the moment, but will be open tomorrow morning.

This is my first brush with the tricky subject of Cultural Appropriation. It makes me rather nervous, but I can only wait until tomorrow to find out what is involved and whether I've transgressed any boundaries.

Back in New Masset, now very hungry after all the walking and the fresh air, I decide I'm too tired to do any cooking and wander up to the diner where I've been told the burger and chips is cheap and very good. I'm not a burger and chips person, but hungry enough to overlook my principles and eat an entire bison if it was put in front of me. The diner is an oblong room with a plywood ceiling and an easy-to-mop tiled floor. There's red plush carpeting stuck to the wall and a row of gilt-framed mirrors hung on it. The tables are wipe-clean and there's a fake brass oil lamp on each one. I'm cheered by the fact that it seems quite popular and there's only one table free.

There are several ways to tell if you're in Canada. Everywhere you go they say "Hello" and "Bonjour" straight away, giving you the choice of French or English, and in restaurants they bring a glass of water to the table as soon as you sit down. The burger, when it comes, is more of a salute to the United States than the UK's fast food industry. It's large, meaty and accompanied by so many chips they fall off the edge of the plate as you try to impale them on the fork. Hungry as I am, I can only eat a fraction and feel I have to apologise to the waitress for my inadequacy as a consumer.

At Copper Beech, I take a quick look at my email and the news headlines before I go to sleep. The Truth and Reconciliation

Commission report has been published today and the figures are as shocking as everyone warned they would be. In the text the word genocide has not just been used explicitly, it has been committed to paper in a government document. Genocide, it seems, is not only a physical act of oppression, it can be carried out over time by policy and ideology.

The report makes depressing reading. At the lowest estimate of death rates (1 in 25, which the report suggests is extremely conservative) children in the residential schools had the same odds of survival as soldiers in the Second World War. But the actual death rate was much higher, because many schools failed to keep comprehensive records and it was established practice to send sick children back to their villages to die in order to make the statistics look healthier. An investigative journalist reported in 1907 that; 'Indian boys and girls are dying like flies... Even war seldom shows as large a percentage of fatalities as does the education system we have imposed on our Indian wards.'[60] In 1913 a government official admitted that '50% of the children who passed through these schools did not live to benefit from their education'.[61] The deputy superintendent for Indian Affairs also admitted that: 'The neglect, abuse, lack of food, isolation from family and badly constructed buildings assisted disease in killing residential school "inmates".' According to the report, at one school 75% of the children died. Things were so bad, a lawyer who conducted a review in 1907 told the government, 'Doing nothing to obviate the preventable causes of death, brings the Department within unpleasant nearness to the charge of manslaughter.'[62] There are 80,000 survivors still alive and entitled to claim compensation for abuse. No wonder so much money has been set aside. But money can't repair the damage that has been done to individuals and to the First Nations as a whole.

Some of the people who worked in the schools were aware of the problems. One of the last letters that Margaret Butcher, nurse and matron of the Haisla children's home in Kitamaat, ever wrote described her experience at summer camp with the children, where they showed her how to collect wild food and live off the land, remembering what their parents and grandparents had taught them. They caught fish and showed Margaret how to strip the bark from trees and eat the soft pulp underneath. Margaret began to recognise that these weeks spent camping in the forest were probably of more use to the children than their enforced indoor regime at the school and she acknowledged that they were also healthier outdoors. 'Camping life is of prime importance in the education of these Indian children. Most of them will spend the greater part of their lives, after school years, in logging or fishing camps … In the Home, routine must be strictly adhered to that the work may be satisfactorily accomplished. Even in play they are restricted in certain measure … but here in Camp their characters have more play, more freedom of expression … and one gets a vision of what could be done were the whole summer, instead of six weeks, spent in this outdoor life … The strained look & weariness of body is lessening & they are laying in a store of health & vigor for the coming session.'

There's a note of disillusionment in Margaret's letter. She never wrote another from Kitamaat, but went back to the school at the end of the summer and gave in her notice. From her last paragraph it seems that she may have been affected by the syndrome all expatriates feared; 'going native'. 'Who would live in a city or who would seek a holiday in some place packed with humans! The writer, for one, will never again be content with crowded life. She is likely to disappear into the wild and be heard of no more.'[63]

Which is exactly what she seems to have done.

12. An Appointment with an Eagle

'All that we say is ours is of Haida Gwaii.
This is our lot, our heritage, our life.'
Guujaaw, *Skidegate Haida Myths and Histories*

I've had a sleepless night. It began to rain sometime around midnight, beating on the veranda roof below my window. The burger was sitting heavily in my stomach, my legs were aching with so much exercise, and I was full of sadness. This whole trip is proving more difficult than I'd anticipated. There's no easy access to anywhere I want to travel and now I have the additional problem of whether I'm going to be allowed to write about it. Will I have to destroy the poems I've already written that mention Haida mythology and history?

It's still early when I get up to make myself a cup of tea in the kitchen. Elle comes in through the door with her Haida spruce-root basket, bringing the smell of damp vegetation, pine resin and ocean fog with her.

"It feels so good," she says. "This place was made for rain."

And it does, it feels beautiful, the air very soft. I can see why you might have a language that has a word for the smell of rain.

Elle makes comfort food for breakfast; pancakes with syrup and preserves. I eat lots of pancakes and drink about a pint of industrial strength coffee. She puts Glenn Gould playing the Goldberg Variations on the stereo. It matches the mood of the weather perfectly. Feeling much more cheerful, I make the decision to give in and hire a car for the next two days, providing of course that they take credit cards. It's the only way I can get up to North Beach and make the most of my time here. The distances are just too great; I'm not keen on hitching lifts and I can't afford taxis.

As I walk over the causeway to what I think is the car hire depot, the tide is out and a lone Raven is figuring out how to excavate a crab almost as large as himself from the mud. I watch him digging it up. The crab is waving its legs frantically, while the Raven expertly turns it over, holds it down with one claw, prizes it apart with his strong beak and crunches it up, bit by bit. The bird looks at me with one bright, black eye as he eats.

At the car hire depot, an elderly man in a beanie is washing a Range Rover. His name is Bert and he is very funny and as chatty as everyone else here. Apparently I've come to the garage where they service the vehicles, so he puts me in the Range Rover and drives me over to the float-plane port where there's a girl hiring out the cars. I would never have guessed where to go. Bert thinks she might have one car left — "Y'see I do the cleaning and the maintenance and I kinda know what they've got out the back". On the way over to the jetty Bert tells me a story about his boss who has just bought a gigantic truck at a car auction. "The first lot they always go — Right! Bang! Just to get the thing going. And my boss he got this truck," Bert points to an outsize Ute with extended wheels and a wrecked front radiator parked on the verge, "and the first thing he did was to run over this drug dealer's car in it. But if you're going to hit a car, best it's a drug dealer!" There's a bit of a hold up as we pull out of the side road — there's a car in front of Bert and a car coming each way on the main road. "Bit of a traffic jam," Bert says in a surprised sort of way. I like being in a place where three cars is a traffic jam.

At the float-plane office they give me an old Dodge which is a bit scratched and worn in places, but it goes and I'd rather have that than one that's pristine and new. I drive into Old Massett, trying to get used to the automatic gearbox and the very soft steering. It yaws around like a boat and sounds like something you might go drag-racing in. Environmentally friendly it is not.

The first thing you notice as you come into Massett is the Royal Canadian Mounted Police headquarters — it's one of the biggest buildings in the village. I feel it's significant that the police station is in Old rather than New Masset. Do the Haida really need more policing than their non-Haida counterparts at the other end of the bay? Today, I'm also seeing more totem poles, possibly because I'm not so tired, but it's possible to cover more ground in the car. Visitors to Copper Beech have told me to look out for Christian White's new Bighouse, so I park up to take a look once I've located it. Christian is one of the younger generation of Haida artists and another of the great grandchildren of Charles Edenshaw. The Bighouse is impressive, built in Haida style with the four big corner beams and cedar planks for walls. There's another being built on the main road, though just the corner and roof posts have been erected so far, and the wall planks are piled outside ready to put in.

I'm not sure where the Band Council office is, so I call in at the small garage to ask and get directed to an imposing modern building on Eagle Road, with two totem poles outside. I speak to a very friendly girl who goes off to consult with someone else at the end of the corridor. She comes back with another woman who tells me that it isn't the Band I need, but the Council of the Haida nation. Fortunately, as it happens, their offices are just down the road, near the fire station. I need to see someone called May Russ, (Haida name Taaw.ga Halaa' Leeyga) who is currently the Chief Administrator of the Haida Nation and a hereditary Chief in her own right.

Russ is a name I keep coming across in my research. The Russ family has played an important part in the history of Haida Gwaii. The name Russ, given to a Haida family who were being 'Anglicised', goes back a long way. In 1877 Amos Russ, a Haida trader from Skidegate who was 'a prince of royal blood, the favourite grandson of the most powerful Chief of his race', married one of Emma Crosby's 'girls' at the school in Port Simpson. Agnes was the daughter of an American man who had settled in Masset and married the daughter of a chief in Old Massett. When Agnes's father went off to the gold fields, the family insisted that the baby be left behind to be brought up by her clan. She appears to have grown into a very strong, spirited woman. When she reached puberty, Agnes was married, according to custom, to a high-ranking man chosen by her family. But the marriage wasn't happy and, when her husband died soon afterwards, Agnes went to Port Simpson and took refuge with the Crosbys to avoid being pushed into another arranged marriage. There she met Amos Russ, who was an early convert to Christianity, and his union with Agnes appears to have been a love match. They both went back to Skidegate as evangelists for their new faith. The Willy Russ who, with his wife Clara, took Emily Carr to Haida Gwaii and showed her the old villages, was probably their son.

Portrait of Mrs Agnes Russ, 1946.
By Mildred Valley Thornton

The elderly woman, 'Old Nanaay', who showed her tattoos to her small grandson and told him, "Boy, that's who you are", was the same Agnes Russ. Her husband Amos was one of the Haida who testified robustly to the McBride-McKenna Commission about the European appropriation of their land. 'The Queen Charlotte Islands are ours. You can see right around the island there are villages and you can see our totem poles, which are the same to us as the white man's pre-emption stakes are to them.' It seems very fitting that it was another Russ, Reynold (Chief Iljawass of Old Massett) who nominated Guujaaw for his position as President of the Haida Nation.

At the Council office, a big, wooden barn of a building, there's a busy hum of activity. There's an important meeting going on. The secretary gives me a seat and tells me that May Russ is in the meeting and won't be out for some time. I could have an appointment next week? But next week I'm in Skidegate and then I'm back to Vancouver. The girl goes off down the corridor into the meeting room and returns about five minutes later. "If you can come back at about half past twelve, she can probably see you for a few minutes." I agree to come back.

Outside I explore a little more of Massett. The primary school is a very Haida construction, with painted symbols on the front wall. There's another decorated building further back, an artist's studio, with an Eagle and a Raven painted in red and black on either side of the door. It looks imposing and there's a totem pole outside. There are two more in the recreation park. It's very encouraging to see so many new totem poles — it seems a symbol of hope.

I walk to the end of the village, where the roads converge and go off into the trees. This is the cemetery, but a notice politely asks non-Haida people not to intrude. It is sacred space and I don't go any further. Tourists don't have a right to go everywhere and see everything, though I would really love to see the new line of graves which accommodate the many sets of human bones recently recovered from museums and private collections and returned to their home territory. The whole community was involved with their funerals, wrapping the remains in cloth, making caskets for the bones, painting symbols on them — all the symbols since it wasn't possible to identify individuals or their moieties. They were interred in the earth with reverence and ceremony. I leave them to sleep in peace and walk back towards the sea.

Old Massett 1900

I'm now at the end of the spit of land where Masset Sound meets the ocean. On the shore, set back a few feet, there's a magnificent totem pole with an eagle perched on top. I know that this is James Hart's pole, carved and raised to celebrate him becoming Chief Edenshaw. Many people regard 'Jim' Hart as one of the most important Haida artists alive today. Beside the totem pole, lying on the grass, are two gigantic cedar tree trunks waiting to be carved. They are old growth, as wide as I'm tall. Under a canopy, Jim Hart is carving a big block of red cedar with two of his apprentices. The air is heavy with the scent of the wood. I stand and watch, too shy to interrupt, though I would love to talk to him about what he's doing — but I live with a sculptor and I know that concentration is everything. They hate interruptions. I'm fascinated by the way that Jim, and the two young men with him, peel back the curls of cedar, deepening and smoothing the shapes they are cutting in the wood. I like watching the rhythm of their hands. They make it look easy, but wood is not an easy substance to work. You have to go with the grain and carve it 'green' before it hardens with age. Cedar has always been very important in Haida art which has used its properties to create unique objects. It is soft to carve, as Bill Reid wrote, 'but of a wonderful firmness' when mature. The sculptor can create very sharp, precise lines and curves. The grain is straight and true, with very few knots and has a beautiful colour when polished — either a glowing amber or a reddish brown. Mature, seasoned wood has a silver patina. The resin in the cedar gives it a long life that resists weathering.

James Hart, Chief Edenshaw's pole in Old Massett

140

It's after one o'clock when May Russ comes out to see me, and the meeting is still going on, so I'm very grateful that she has made the time for me at such short notice. She's a plump, dark woman with an air of quiet confidence; very businesslike, but with a warm personality. I outline my project as quickly and simply as I can. She tells me that yes, I do need permission to write about the Haida Nation and their history. If I put it all in an email to her, she will forward it on to the Culture Committee for their consideration. I thank her for her time and she goes back into the meeting room.

This situation seems quite odd to a westerner, since I can write about the history of any other nation anywhere in the world without asking permission. But I've been thinking about it all night and I can understand that a people who have had every other aspect of their culture, their land and their basic human rights taken away, might be very sensitive about the appropriation, or even the borrowing, of what they have left.

When Robert Bringhurst first published *A Story as Sharp as a Knife*, a scholarly work which gave status to Haida Literature as one of the great literary traditions of the world, he became the target of an unexpected backlash. Although not First Nation himself, he had been studying their language and literature for a long time and was a great friend of Bill Reid. He was working with the original transcripts of the Haida stories, dictated to an anthropologist called John Swanton a hundred years earlier, by the original 'owners' of the stories. They had the right to tell them and they passed them on to Swanton. Many would see this as 'permission' both implied and explicit for written versions of these stories.

Bringhurst studied the Haida language in order to complete his translations and he made the texts available for any Haida who didn't speak their language (of which there are many) and for all Canadians as a body of literature that pre-dated their imported European tradition, and also for the rest of the world, as one of the great literary traditions, equalling the oral poetry of the Greeks. But the backlash was severe — when Bringhurst began to recite one of the poems in Haida during a public lecture, a girl was so appalled she had to run outside and vomit.

In the second edition of the book, Bringhurst felt he had to write a new 'political afterword' as a rebuttal. In it he admits that 'the fact that I was reading and celebrating this inheritance as literature was exciting to Bill Reid, but to many other Haida it has seemed misguided at best... to some especially perverse and intrusive.' Bringhurst also understood why. 'People whose culture and identity have been relentlessly squeezed over more than a century, and then, with equal mindlessness, romanticized and commercialized for the tourist trade, are entitled to be angry and suspicious ... But the view that no outsider should speak of the Haida mythtellers without Haida permission is not the view I was taught by my Haida teacher and not a view to which I subscribe.'

Debbie Reese, a First Nation professor of Indian studies, puts the other view, pointing out not just the cultural divide, but also the issue of gender. 'Come on guys! You've had 200 years of misrepresenting us.'[64] There is, she says, a lack of accurate portrayal of First Nation culture in books and films which contributes to the disengagement and subsequent drop-out rate of young people in schools. First Nation women get a particularly raw deal. I agree with that. Before I travelled I read as much as I could about Haida Gwaii and about Canadian indigenous people in general and watched whatever films and documentaries I could get hold of. One of them is a silent film made by Edward S. Curtis, who took some wonderful photographs in the first two decades of the twentieth century. His film (which is also a book), *In the Land of the Head Hunters,* masquerades as documentary, but is actually a film director's fantasy about the lives of west coast indigenous people complete with kidnapped princesses, head hunters, evil shamans and love-sick princes. It contrasts sharply with the more modern *The 8th Fire,* which is a documentary about the contemporary plight of First Nation Canadians made by the First Nation Canadians themselves and which is electrifying.

At the beginning of the twentieth century, anthropologists flocked to the reservations to record the stories of what they believed to be a dying culture. They transcribed the stories that were dictated to them, but not always accurately. Sometimes the texts were even rewritten to fit European ideas of literature and storytelling. 'In a few instances,' one author admits, 'due to a lack of refinement of thought in the original stories, I have taken some license in their transcription'.[65] History, as the saying goes, is always written by the victors in any conflict. Like the films, most of the early books were written by Europeans from their own point of view and with the most appallingly patronising tone. 'The unsophisticated aboriginal of British Columbia is almost a memory of the past. He leaves no permanent monument, no ruins of former greatness'.[66] The knowledge of their authors is often shallow and the point of view relentlessly biased towards European, Christian ideals. But things changed in the second half of the twentieth century, when First Nation people, encouraged by anthropologists and scholars, began to record their own memoirs. You get a much more accurate account of daily life in the reservations from the autobiographies of Chief James Sewid of Alert Bay, or Florence Edenshaw Davidson from Massett. They tell their own stories fluently and with authority. It is more than time to turn the narrative over to the indigenous people themselves. But should that prevent anyone else writing about them?

Then there's the question of copyright. I believe in ethical research and I am perfectly happy with the idea that certain stories, songs and dances are owned by particular people — we have copyright for written material in the west and there's no reason why oral traditions shouldn't be similarly protected. These cultural artefacts are passed on like heirlooms. I feel the same way about my own family stories, but I don't see why other people shouldn't write about me and my family, provided that the stories are properly attributed and I am free to raise my voice in dissent if I don't like the view taken. In our society people are free to write about me, even without my permission. But should that be the situation? Should we allow that? There are so many questions.

If the strict view of cultural appropriation was taken then I wouldn't be free to write about anything but my own cultural inheritance — Greek mythology would be out of bounds, and no one who lived outside Stratford on Avon would be allowed to comment on Shakespeare. Shakespeare would never have been allowed to write his plays, whose plots were stolen from other people's stories in the first place. Taken to its logical conclusion it would also prevent non-native people from having tattoos — a friend I know has a beautiful Haida raven on her shoulder, though she is not of the raven moiety. We shouldn't, technically, buy any tourist souvenirs with Haida designs, or masks or any of the other native regalia on sale in the museum shops. It would also prevent me from writing poems about any aspect of Haida life and culture and this journal would be similarly proscribed. This is a very complex subject.

I send an email to the Council of the Haida Nation asking for permission.[67]

The Moss Forest, Tow Hill Road, Masset

Afterwards I take my packed lunch of sandwiches and filtered water and drive up Tow Hill Road, northwards, into the Naikoon reserve towards Agate Beach. It's stopped raining and the vegetation is steaming in the warm, afternoon sun. The track to Tow Hill is a graded dirt road between fir trees that grow, like the walls of a green canyon, on either side. Today they are wreathed in mist rising from the forest floor underneath, which is thick with sphagnum moss, a deep, soft growth that muffles the shapes of rocks and fallen logs, turning them into surreal green objects. The trees too are coated in a second skin of moss and their branches look as though they've had green quilts wrapped round them. The moss is so thick it drips from the tips of the branches like candlewax. In this moss forest there is almost complete silence as the moss absorbs any sound like deep snow. Around me, the trees assume strange shapes and green disguises. I imagine that at night, in moonlight, they would seem surreal and threatening.

I turn off the track where a board indicates Agate Beach and park on the edge of the pebble slope. I'm the only person here. Out of the car I sit on a driftwood tree trunk and eat my sandwiches, listening to the 'long, withdrawing roar' of the sea on the shingle, the low detonations and the crash of pebble on pebble. It's worth bumping up a dirt road for miles, just to sit here. The waves are spectacular, unlike the calm blue waters off Vancouver Island and Alert Bay. I've been told that the ocean here has a thirty-two foot tidal range twice a day. That's a powerful tide.

Out there, somewhere in the deep waters, are the big beasts of the ocean — the Orca and humpback whales. The latter were hunted almost to extinction by the whaling fleets that arrived with the colonists. Coastal First Nation people had always hunted whales, using big canoes with a cleft prow to balance their wooden harpoons. But they killed only a few, seasonally, to fill their own needs. It wasn't the mass slaughter for commercial purposes that came with the Europeans. Since whale hunting has been limited by international agreement the humpback numbers have been growing, but now there are new threats. As fish stocks become more and more depleted, it's not only humans that have been unable to find the fish they once relied on for a living. A young humpback washed up onshore here recently had an empty stomach and intestines and apparently died of starvation. These islands, once known as 'the Galapagos of the North', are gradually emptying of the rich diversity of wildlife they were famous for. As I watch the waves roll in, I realise that I'm unlikely to see the flick of a whale's tail or the black and white flash of a pod of Orca in the wild, unless I'm incredibly lucky, or go on a paid tourist whale hunt, locating them by ultrasound. But I've experienced that elsewhere and, although there is something magical about being next to a breeching whale, being on a boat full of people shrieking "Look!" and "There she blows!" in a parody of Moby Dick, brandishing telephoto lenses and I-phones, takes something away from it. To encounter an animal in the wild by accident, rather than design, is a different kind of experience.[68]

After I've eaten I walk up the beach looking for agates. This coast is famous for them and they are often washed up by the storm tides. I don't know exactly what I'm looking for, but find a few pebbles of cloudy amber. These go in my pocket with other small stones of different colours. There are dark green and vivid red jaspers, polished by the constant tumbling action of the ocean, and satiny black ones that look like argillite — a kind of slate that only occurs on these islands. Haida carvers have always been skilled at carving it into plates and dishes, intricately decorated.

The tide has turned and is coming in now. The waves are beginning to crash and thud with much more energy, surging up the gradient to foam at my feet. This is one of the most treacherous coasts in the world for shipping and is littered with shipwrecks. The body of water in front of me has travelled an immense distance across the Pacific, generating a lot of energy, and, when it finally hits land, complex currents are created. Storms coming off the deep, warm waters of the Pacific regularly reach hurricane force. This coast also runs along the Pacific Rim tectonic plate which regularly heaves the sea onshore after seismic tremors. Waves of more than ninety feet high have been recorded and the terrain makes any kind of rescue extremely difficult. A passenger ferry, the Queen of the North, which was wrecked in 2006 south of Prince Rupert, is still at the bottom of the ocean, leaking fuel, beyond the reach of salvage. And people here are still observing the consequences of the 1989 Exxon Valdez tanker wreck, which spilled approximately thirty million US gallons of oil into the ocean further north in Prince William Sound.

So I can see why the 'No Enbridge' local residents are totally against the idea of an oil terminal on the mainland, at Kitamaat, to transport the tar-sands oil to other locations by ship. The tankers would have to sail up past the northern end of Haida Gwaii in order to get out into the deep ocean, negotiating one of the most dangerous channels anywhere in the world, described as 'a malevolent weather factory' where a 'unique combination of wind, tide, shoals, and shallows produces a kind of destructive synergy that has few parallels elsewhere in nature'.[69] The coastlines of mainland British Columbia and the islands of Haida Gwaii are very fragile. Enbridge's Northern Gateway pipeline project and the associated oil tanker port threaten the Great Bear rainforest and some of the most pristine wildlife habitats on earth. An oil spill would be a catastrophe, destroying fisheries, salmon rivers, the coastal habitats of the grizzlies and the rare Spirit Bears, as well as breeding colonies of sea lions, otters, and the health of an ocean where humpback whales are only just beginning to return after being hunted almost to extinction. All coastal First Nation people are opposed to Enbridge in a huge display of solidarity. I've just read a report in the local paper that the Lax Kwalaams Band, on the mainland near Prince Rupert, have turned down an offer of about C$267,000 each to allow a natural gas pipeline through their land. That is big money by anyone's standard. The Band Chief is quoted as saying that, 'This is not a money issue: this is environmental and cultural.'[70]

How do we protect the planet from ourselves? That's one of the questions I came here to try to answer. On the bookshelves at Copper Beech, I found an extraordinary document which sets out the Haida vision for the future. It also points up the great flaw in our relationship to the environment. I hadn't really thought of the fact that the constitutions of our own, supposedly developed, countries set out the rights and obligations of individuals and government to each other, but totally ignore the rights of the natural world and our obligations to it. This relationship is fundamental to our lives, but it seems that only the indigenous people recognise its importance. As Ian Gill, president of Eco-trust Canada points out, 'The framers of most national constitutions had no words for the land or people's relationship to it.'[71] We can invoke Habeus Corpus, Magna Carta, the 5th Amendment, or the right to carry a gun, but there is nothing in our constitutions about protecting the earth, the sea or the sky that we depend on for our very existence.

But the Haida have something unique. On Susan Musgrave's bookshelf, looking for bedtime reading, I found a copy of the Haida Land Use Vision, which embodies the Haida principle of *Yah'guudang*, which translates as 'respect for all living things'. It's a humbling document full of profound wisdom about the natural world and our place in it and it sets out the complex interactions between every element; the relationships between trees and salmon and bears and humans, between land and air and ocean. An eco-system is a delicate balance of inter-actions between every part of it. The Haida Land Use Vision lists the catastrophic effects of only a hundred years of mismanagement which have been enough to upset thousands of years of careful co-existence. The decline in the salmon population in British Columbia is only one element of concern in a document that lists dozens, and the document sets out the chain of causation.

Clear-cut logging in Haida Gwaii

The Haida Land Use Vision describes how the environment, due to unregulated human activity, becomes unstable and eventually unable to support wildlife. Logging is one of the culprits. 'As a watershed becomes progressively logged, the qualities that make for a healthy salmon stream become degraded.' Commercial clear-cut logging leaves the land exposed. 'Seasonal floods run faster and higher, ripping away the structure of logs and spawning pools and the shelter of small side channels. Roads and bridge-crossings funnel sediments into the streams. Landslides and debris torrents are catastrophic events that effectively erase a stream's capacity to provide habitat'.[72] The document lists nine major rivers that are almost barren of salmon now. And with the disappearing salmon the fertility of the soil goes too. I hadn't realised that the bears and eagles used to take the dying salmon into the woods to eat, leaving a large part of the carcasses to decompose and create nutrients for plants and trees. In places where the salmon runs have failed, there are no bears, no eagles and the forests are less fertile, the leaf litter poor in terms of microbes and other nutrients. Every part of the ecology depends on every other part.

This is one of the most important things I've read since I arrived here and part of what I hoped for when I came. It is a blueprint for responsible, respectful, sustainable life on the planet. The Haida are right; what we need is a constitution for the land, sea and sky, to protect them from predation and pollution, one that would bind all governments and all people.

Sitting here, alone on the edge of the forest, listening to the ocean and watching the waves heave and break on the pebble beach, feels like being in paradise. It is a healing experience. But I can't help wondering if it is possible to find true peace for the soul while so many people, and the environment, are suffering such appalling abuse. Shouldn't we be getting angry and calling for action, making things happen, rather than sneaking off into the wilderness to get in touch with our inner selves? It seems to me rather like a priest going into retreat in the middle of a massacre, to pray about it, rather than going out there to stand in line and stop it happening. I'm beginning to feel that I need to engage more actively with these environmental issues. Thinking and talking, even donating money, is all very well, but perhaps some doing needs to be done too even if that means taking risks. But what can I do that would be effective and useful?

13. The Edge of the World

'— my hopes and dreams for the future are that my children, my future grandchildren, and their grandchildren will be able to go out on the low tide, harvest clams, cockles, mussels, abalone, herring roe on kelp, and continue to live as we are, on the bounties of the ocean.'
(Diane Brown, An Ocean Forum for Haida Gwaii, Jan. 2009)

There's a new group of people at Copper Beech this morning. Colette and her friend Julia, with their sons Ben and Chris, arrived yesterday. They've come from Vancouver to research Haida art with a view to buying some pieces for the institution that they represent. It's also a birthday trip for one of the boys. I'm still amazed by the friendliness of people here. We sit over breakfast talking about Haida mythology, our travels, things we like, sharing our personal stories. I talk about my experience at the Vancouver Art Gallery and they tell me that the gallery in fact has a big collection of indigenous art, but doesn't have the space to show it — a situation that will be resolved when the new gallery is built. Colette and Julia had been to see Jim Hart yesterday afternoon, while I was at Agate Beach, and had a long talk about the carving that he's doing as well as Haida art generally. Apparently he was very helpful. They think I should have introduced myself yesterday, and I do regret not having had the courage to approach him, but I'm aware that the Hart family has recently been bereaved and this has made me reluctant to intrude without an introduction. I've written nine biographies and interviewed hundreds of people, but I still feel a deep reserve about pushing my way into other people's lives.

Today I've planned an early start to drive up to North Beach. I know that I can't make it all the way to Rose Spit and back in one day, but I intend to get as far as I can towards the northernmost tip of Haida Gwaii. I pack my small rucksack with food and water, a light rain proof and my walking boots.

The early morning sea fog is still drifted in around the trees as I drive up Tow Hill Road. It's eerie and rather magical. The road grader is out today, so I have to negotiate the newly ploughed surface around it, spitting up stones under the hire car. At least I ticked the Collision Damage Waiver box on the insurance certificate. But there is a stern warning in the paperwork that taking the vehicle off-road invalidates the insurance and there's a thousand dollar fine for retrieval if you get stuck.

When I reach the end of the track at North Beach the knowledge of that fine is frustrating, because the notices beside the track make it clear that you can drive up the hard sand for quite a long way if you've got your own car and you know the tides. The Dodge is sturdy and quite capable of it. I've driven on sand dunes in the Middle East and the beach looks an easy ride. It's very tempting just to follow the other wheel tracks out of the forest down onto the sand. I think about it, but in the end common sense and the reality of the fine win out. I park the car next to the self-catering log cabins and walk.

Where the river enters the sea, just below Tow Hill, the carcasses of trees washed up by the high spring tides are submerged in the sand like shipwrecks. The tide is out at the moment and there's a wide expanse of sand dotted with utes. The vehicles on the edge of the sea look very small. Distances are deceptive here — much greater than they seem. Beside each parked vehicle is a figure digging in the sand, harvesting something.

As I begin to walk up the beach, I see familiar figures. It's Colette, Julia and the boys from Copper Beech. They too are walking to the edge of the world. But then I see the boys stop one of the fishermen's utes as it drives past. There's a conversation with the driver and then they wave me over. Would I like a lift to the far end of North Beach? The fisherman, whose name is Randy, will take us all for C$50. So, of course I say yes and heave myself into the back of the truck with the boys and several buckets of razor clams. That's what the men are digging up out of the sand. The clams are several inches long and the pale, fleshy tongues loll out of the narrow shells across the plastic edges of the containers.

Razor Clams, North Beach, Masset

It's a long drive up North Beach and Randy can't take us all the way. Eventually the beach becomes too soft, the drifts of pebbles too unstable and there's a danger of the ute getting bogged down. I'm a bit disappointed, but at least I'm nearer to my goal than I could have achieved on foot. When I look back, Tow Hill looks small in the distance. Randy says he can only give us an hour or so before the rising tide begins to cause problems and he needs to be back to sell his clams.

I would love to walk up to Rose Spit, which I can now see, and discuss it with Randy, but he says it would be another two hours walk and then I'd have to walk all the way back — the whole twenty two kilometres and not easy walking on shifting shingle and soft sand, because the tide would be in and there wouldn't be any hard sand left to walk on. He's not happy about me doing it on my own either — once the fishermen leave as the tide rises, the beach will be deserted. I allow myself to be convinced. But I intend to get as far as I can northward, before Randy's curfew.

The sand is a beachcomber's dream. On my right, on the edge of the forest, which is beginning to thin out now, there's a complex barricade of tree trunks bleached to a pale silver by sun and sea. There are fragments of net and bits of polystyrene, but much less detritus than I'd expected. The sea is relatively clean here. Under my feet is another narrative. There are long tubes with a circular bulb at the end — some of them almost a foot in diameter. This is a kind of kelp, which I've read that the Haida used to cure and then use as a storage vessel for fish oil when they were travelling. The bulbs are perfectly circular, like soft suede to the touch, and quite beautiful.

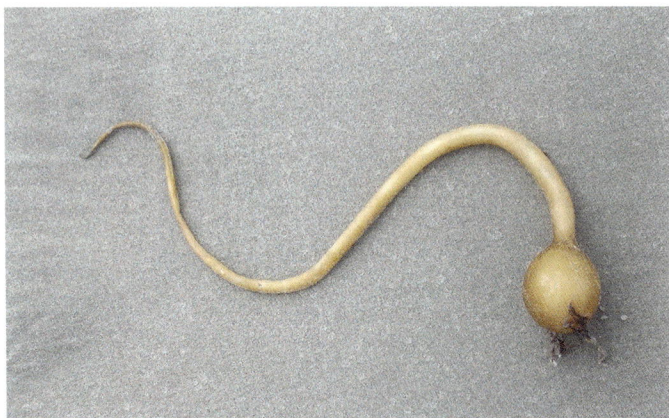

Bulb Kelp, North Beach, Masset

Further on there's a dead crab, upside down, the claws delicately arranged on either side, as if for a scientific drawing. Not far away are the neat hoof marks of a deer, fresh from its morning walk. There are hundreds of clam shells, most pecked to pieces by birds, but I'm lucky enough to find one that is intact, half buried in the sand, the soft flesh gone, but still hinged. It's huge and I tuck it carefully into my rucksack wondering if I can get it back to England without breaking it.

The perfect clam shell is a symbolic find and it fills me with joy. From here I can look up and see the curve of Rose Spit — an arc of sand that goes out into the ocean, separating the Pacific from the northern end of the Hecate Strait. It was the first piece of land to rise up out of the sea in Haida mythology, and it is where the Raven found human beings, little Haida, in a clam shell and tempted them to come out.

The most wonderful thing about Haida myths and stories is that they are so firmly connected to the landscape. They are rooted in it, originating from a relationship with the land that goes back more than ten thousand years. The Haida are steeped in their own mythology just as we westerners are steeped in Greek mythology — the difference is that the mythology is their own and relates to the landscape around them. We make references to Helen of Troy, the Trojan Horse, but they're just stories, distilled into metaphor, not relevant to our own history and environment. Here, the Haida mythology means something; they're looking at it. In the words of Guujaaw, 'our culture is our relationship to the land. That's where our songs come from, that's where our language comes from…' It's the fabric and setting of the stories that are handed on from generation to generation. Even their traditional dances 'are all about the creatures that we share this land with'.[73]

One of my bedtime books at the moment, borrowed from the Copper Beech bookshelves, is a series of archaeological papers on Haida Gwaii.[74] Archaeologists have been astonished to find that their research has borne out stories told by the Haida for centuries. Some of the 'myths' feature grizzly bears, which don't live on Haida Gwaii, but then the archaeologists found grizzly bear bones in a cave on the islands and realised that they were there once, when Haida Gwaii was connected to the mainland, before the sea rose at the end of the last ice age. In the book, archaeologist Daryl Fedje states firmly that, 'People have lived in this archipelago for at least 12,800 years … They saw their climate change over millennia, and sea levels rise high over their grandparents' villages and then fall back so that new villages could be built on their ancestors' fishing grounds … The Haida people have been part of a long-term process of environmental transformation and cultural change.' The stories are just one more proof that the Haida had been there at that time.

There are other stories too, which have recently been verified by archaeological research. In some of the older stories, there's mention of a land without trees, where people had to sleep in caves and there was grass everywhere. This too is a description of Haida Gwaii's landscape, newly revealed by the retreating ice, before the waters rose. In an oral culture, a people's history is recorded in its stories and the narrative handed down from generation to generation. Mythology conceals important truths.

The existence of this mythology and the legacy of story that has been handed on, is part of the First Nation evidence for their 'ownership' of the land they have occupied and depended on for so many thousands of years. One Elder, questioned by government officials about his clan's rights to the territory, asked them bluntly: 'If this is your land, where are your stories?' And then he began to tell a story in his own language, to demonstrate his people's knowledge of the landscape and the longevity of their traditions.[75] Such oral evidence was never taken seriously by the colonial administration.

I've gone as far north as I can go now, without missing my assignation with Randy to be driven back. I walk down to where the incoming waves have washed the sand glass-smooth. I am standing on the edge of the world, looking out over Dixon's Entrance to the Pacific with Alaska somewhere to the north of me and southwest, across unimaginable distances, Australasia. There is only the sea for thousands of miles. This is the biggest body of water on the planet and the deepest, its unhindered tides driven by the lunar engine, with an energy felt nowhere else. It is one of the most powerful forces on earth. I'm conscious of a strange yearning as I look out across the water. Perhaps it was that — some kind of primitive curiosity, a longing to know what was there — that drove the first people to put to sea in flimsy canoes and risk their lives to find new places to live.

As I walk back to where Randy has parked his ute, the wind is beginning to strengthen and there are clouds out to sea. There's

North Beach, looking towards Rose Spit

going to be a storm, Randy tells me when I arrive. He says there's been a lot of them this spring and he dreads the El Nino that's developing, because there will be no crabs and the halibut will be scarce. Last time there was an El Nino the catches were down by half. This time, because it's going to be a big one, maybe even down by two thirds. Randy's wearing a silver whale around his neck on a chain, one of his clan symbols. It means that he's a member of the Raven moiety and the whale is his crest.

Randy tells me that he usually works on one of the big fishing boats. "That's my boat," he says, pointing to one of the fishing vessels off shore. "But it's good to feel the ground under my feet for a while." He's on shore for two weeks. We stand together looking out to sea, waiting for the others and he suddenly says, very simply; "I was born and raised here. This is my place."

I wonder what it must feel like to belong in that way — to know your ancestors have been there for ten thousand years, that every bit of your culture, your genetic make-up, is rooted in this landscape, this place. If you're of the Eagle moiety you look up at the Bald Eagles spreading their wings overhead and know you belong just as they belong. If you are a Raven, you look a Raven in

156

the eye every day of your life, and their kronk kronk is as familiar as your own language. Randy belongs to a particular landscape, in a way I will never be able to and I envy that.

Two years ago, about this time of year, I was sitting on an Iron Age hilltop fort in the Scottish Highlands, watching the sun rise across a vast expanse of the wilderness that is Sutherland. It's probably the only place on earth where I can say for sure that my ancestors lived more than two millennia ago. That's because I'm a mongrel, the offspring of migrants. My mother's father was from a family that came from Genoa in Italy, but her mother was Scottish, a product of the Highland Clearances. Sutherland is our family name. My cousin is formidable in full highland regalia when he comes to family occasions. On the other side, my father's family were Irish, from both north and south, some of them from an area of Ireland that was colonised by the Vikings when they first came down the west coast of Britain. My father's corn-coloured hair and Norse blue eyes marked him out as one of them, in a family that was otherwise dark haired, white skinned and Celtic.

I was born and brought up in England with this mixed genetic heritage, the pull of wild Sutherland running in my blood alongside a lot of Irish blarney, Nordic reserve and Mediterranean hedonism. There is a sense that, in Europe, 'we are all migrants'. Even the Haida came from somewhere else originally — thousands of years ago they migrated across the Pacific, perhaps from Asia, possibly Melanesia, probably a mix of all these. No-one knows exactly and there are lots of theories.

Randy drops me about half way down the beach so that I can walk some of the way back. I eat my lunch sitting on a tree trunk gazing out over a great emptiness. The fishing boats and the clam diggers have gone and there's only the ocean, the sky and me. A big wind is beginning to get up with driving squalls of rain. Cloud formations are streaming inland above me and there are sand wraiths twisting and swirling along the beach, blowing sand into everything, including my eyes. I'm reluctant to leave North Beach, but the wind makes it uncomfortable to stay. Storms happen quickly here. As I bump the Dodge down Tow Hill Road the tree tops are threshing on either side of the track.

Randy's Ute, North Beach, Masset

There's a woman staying at Copper Beech whose Haida birth mother has died. She was adopted as a baby, by a couple in Toronto, and has only seen her birth mother twice before, after tracing her with some difficulty. Carol, though that's not her real name, was one of the victims of the 'Sixties Scoop' — the policy pursued through the sixties and seventies, of removing children from their First Nation mothers and placing them with white, non-indigenous couples to be brought up as 'proper Canadians'. It was just another way of trying to 'kill the Indian in the child' and it caused just as much heartache and suffering as other policies with the same aim. Carol had never been told of her Haida heritage and, when she traced her birth-mother, found it difficult to connect. She is devastated that her mother has died before they could form a proper relationship.

Elle is taking care of Carol and has been to the funeral with her this afternoon while I was at the beach. The service was in the church at Old Massett, Christian but with a Haida carved casket with her mother's clan identity painted on it, the singing of traditional songs, and several women from her family as proxy pall-bearers. This is a new development in the combining of Haida and Christian culture. The women's names were read out during the service and they stood beside the casket, although they didn't physically carry it. Elle found it very moving. Afterwards there was a modern 'potlatch' for the funeral.

Carol says that her life has been transformed by the ceremony. She has been presented with her own clan regalia by the family, formally accepted into it and given her Haida name. Carol says that she feels surrounded by love and is quite prepared to take charge of her own Haida identity. "I know now that I belong *here*," she says, emphasising the last word quietly, but firmly. "This is who I am." She's going to investigate moving here as soon as she can. The Haida have a matriarchal society, so Carol's status is defined by her mother and she may have the right to live on land that is still termed 'reservation' territory. This was complicated by the Colonial administration who imposed their own, patriarchal, culture on the Haida. Women had to take their husband's names on marriage and, if they married a European, they lost their right to 'Indian' status (an advantage in colonial eyes but a tragedy for their own communities as they could not return to their villages if the relationship broke down). If Carol's birth father is also Haida, she will be able to live in Old Massett.

It's my last night here, for the time being, and I've decided to treat myself to a meal at the restaurant just along the road from Copper Beech. It's called Charters and it isn't open every night, but is enthusiastically recommended by everyone. It's fully booked, but fortunately there is a tiny table in a corner that can accommodate one person. The atmosphere is lively and the staff are friendly and welcoming. Tantalising smells escape from the kitchen door whenever it opens. The menu has me salivating before I've got past the first courses. I order locally caught scallops with Masset smoked salmon, followed by braised chicken and, for pudding, the legendary chocolate mousse. Puddings are definitely my Achilles heel when it comes to healthy eating.

As I'm eating my scallops the door opens and Elle comes in with Carol. They immediately ask me to eat with them, but a table for two can't, because of problems with space, be made into a table for three. Charters is so popular it's crammed. Then Colette and Julia and the boys arrive and a similar invitation is offered. They have a bigger table, so, as soon as I've finished eating, I join them for coffee. Apparently they've been back to see Jim Hart and he says that he would like to meet me. But he and his wife are off to Vancouver tomorrow morning early and I'm heading down to Skidegate, so I will have to see if we can arrange something for the following week before I, too, have to leave for Vancouver.

My timing is terrible. Another contact, Terri-Lynn Williams Davidson, the Haida lawyer and musician, is also away giving a concert in Vancouver, accompanied by her husband, artist Robert Davidson, while I'm here. I would have liked to talk to both of them. But my timing was dictated by a course I wanted to attend, on First Nation Mythology, originally arranged on one of the islands off Vancouver. I booked my flights and my trip to Haida Gwaii well in advance to take advantage of a cheap deal and then, a couple of weeks before I left, the course was cancelled. It was too late to cancel the flights, but it did give me an extra week to explore the islands and, as a result, my work in progress has changed. I came to finish a collection of poetry, based on Haida mythology, their environmental concerns and the landscape of the islands, not to research Haida social history. I came to write poems, not the book I appear to be writing. My travel journal has somehow morphed into something else. And the poems? I've written a few — it's not something you can force. And I've had good news; my sequence of poems on the life of Emily Carr has been accepted by an eco-magazine called *Earthlines*, and a small poetry publisher has expressed interest in the collection when it's finished.

We all walk back to Copper Beech together in the wind and the rain. I creep into Margaret Atwood's bed and try to sleep in spite of the big northwesterly storm beating against my bedroom window.

160

14. The Spirit in the Blood

'I was a baby boy still in the womb when I dreamed this singing.
It was given me by the Ravens. Now I am a man but have not
forgotten it. I dreamed it before I ever was born… no one else
sings like this, for it was I that dreamed it myself.'
Pamich's story, as transcribed by Alfred L. Kroeber

When I wake up everything is quiet. The storm has passed over and there's a hint of sunlight behind the cloudy sky. It's another departure morning. Carol is returning to Toronto to unmake her life; Colette and Julia are leaving for Skidegate, and so am I. There are affectionate farewells with Elle, whose presence in the house has been such a calm and peaceful influence. Carol is planning to return to Haida Gwaii as soon as she can organise it. I'm returning next week before my flight back to Vancouver.

I'm keeping the car because I've been unable to get a room at a B&B called Jags Beanstalk. This coffee shop and bistro, with its associated accommodation, is run by a Haida family. It's in the centre of Skidegate, casual and quirky and very, very popular — it's been totally booked out for months and there are no cancellations. So instead I'm in a guest house called Haida House at Tlaal — several kilometres north of Skidegate, in the woods at the mouth of the Tlell River on the edge of the Hecate Strait. On the internet it looks remote and beautiful, but there's no public transport.

It takes no time at all to pack my bags and a picnic lunch into the Dodge and drive across the inlet, turning right this time, away from North Beach, towards Queen Charlotte village at the extreme southern end of Graham Island. There's no possibility of getting lost, no need for maps. This is the only road there is. It's called the Yellowhead Highway and it's at the extreme northern end of the Trans-Canada highway which goes all the way from Masset, via a few ferries and the Yellowhead Pass across the Rockies, continuing for nearly three thousand kilometres, through four states, until it reaches Winnipeg. Fortunately for me, Skidegate is a mere one hundred kilometres down the road, but I love the sense that I could drive almost forever across the continent if I kept going.

Once out of Masset I stop at Pure Lake for a break. Elle has told me about this beautiful swimming hole. After a short walk through the trees I discover a round, clear lake mirroring the sky in the centre of the forest. No sound but birds and the distant roar of a logging lorry on the road. The lake is quite gloomy today because the sky is overcast and the water level is low because of the drought. It's too cold to swim, so I sit at one of the picnic tables provided and drink some coffee from the flask and eat some of Elle's cake.

When I walk back to the road I find two other cars just drawing up to park behind mine. Pure Lake is a beauty spot. So far I've found nowhere that is completely wild; not one place where there hasn't been the sound of human beings or picnic tables, waste disposal sites, log cabins, marked trails, bush toilets. This landscape has been carefully curated for human beings. North Beach was the wildest, once the clam diggers had left. But I still have a longing for the wilderness — not just beautiful scenery — and I begin to wonder if I will ever find it. On my own, without camping gear, I can't get far enough off the beaten track.

About half way down the highway I turn off to take a look at Port Clements, an old logging settlement on Masset Inlet. It's small; just a few wooden houses, a church, a shop, a logging museum and some industrial sheds. There's a café which appears to be closed and a long wooden jetty going out into the middle of the Inlet. A logging barge is tied up to it and I walk out to take a look. The size of this saltwater inland lake is impressive. The amazing thing is that it is still surrounded by trees. Logging is part of the human history of Haida Gwaii and it's really the only means of making a living in Port Clement. The tourist season is short and not lucrative enough to make it the primary means of subsistence for residents.Once there were fourteen logging stations around Masset Inlet and a gigantic sawmill that could cut up to 150,000 planks a day. The massive cedars, hemlocks and spruce of the old-growth forest were much in demand in the rest of North America. The spruce was particularly prized for aircraft manufacture during World War I and afterwards because of its strength to weight ratio. During World War II the Mosquito fighter-bomber still had a frame made from spruce. By the sixties and seventies the dearth of big trees left in other locations made Haida Gwaii timber particularly valuable. The loggers moved into the old-growth forest in droves. Clear cut logging changed the landscape irrevocably.

Port Clements' timber wharf

The Haida, for whom the trees were an important part of their culture, watched the destruction with despair. But it was Guujaaw, in the mid nineteen eighties, who decided that the time had come for action. The site chosen to confront the logging

163

companies was Lyell Island, off the coast of the southern island of Moresby, where old-growth forest was still intact. The tactics were old-fashioned obstruction, manning the barricades despite physical intimidation and the risk of injury. So strong was the feeling throughout the Haida community that eventually even the Elders — dignified men and women in their sixties, seventies and eighties — came to join the protest and stand with their children and grandchildren to defy the logging companies. Meanwhile Guujaaw and the Haida lawyers, including a very young Terri-Lynn Williams Davidson, also fought a battle in the courts to establish Haida rights. In the logging blockade they were up against 'the whole economic system' of Canada. "We needed a cutting edge," Guujaaw said. "That cutting edge was title."[77] In the absence of written records and deeds, much of the Haida title was embedded in the totems that staked their claims to abandoned villages and evidenced in their stories; myths and histories that went thousands of years back in time. The Haida's entire culture is rooted in the land. And in the end the law was on the side of the Haida. In their arrogance and conviction of superiority, the early colonial administrators had neglected to get the Haida to sign any papers or contract documents transferring their rights to the land. After all, if you don't believe there are any rights to give, why bother to get anyone to sign papers? It was one oversight their descendants have lived to regret.

Lyell Island was a significant victory, and eventually, in 2004, legislation was enacted which means that no logging can take place on Haida Gwaii without consultation with, and the agreement of, the Council of the Haida Nation. The ruling went further than just Haida Gwaii, as the Supreme Court of Canada ruled unanimously 'that governments have a legal duty to consult with Aboriginals before allowing logging, mining, new roads and other development on Crown land that is subject to Native land claims.' Chief Justice Beverley McLachlin stated that, 'the Crown, acting honourably, cannot cavalierly run roughshod over Aboriginal interests where claims affecting those interests are being seriously pursued.' The ruling gives the First Nations a measure of control over what happens on their land, though the principle is now being severely tested by the fossil fuel companies trying to build pipelines to transport oil from the Alberta Tar Sands. The line of confrontation is now the Pacific Gateway Pipeline, proposed by Enbridge, and which the current government have approved.

There's a small mining museum in Port Clements that has preserved some of the old donkey engines and chain saws, as well as more homely objects used by the settlers. These include a cast-iron boot last, for the endless footwear repairs that were necessary, a hand-operated sewing machine that would have got a lot of use in a place where you had to make your own clothes as well as sew your own bed and table linen, and a wooden washing machine that was once state of the art for the colonial housewife. The museum also records the collision between the human population and native wildlife. There's a photograph recording the last caribou to be shot on the islands in 1908. Since then, no-one has seen a caribou on Haida Gwaii. In one corner, perched on a rock, are the stuffed remains of the rare white raven, cocking a carefully placed glass eye towards the visitor. The white raven, an almost mythical creature in Port Clements, was killed by an encounter with an electricity pylon in 2005.

Port Clements was also the site of the fabled Golden Spruce, known to the Haida as *K'iid K'yaas*. It was a rare genetic mutation of the more common Sitka Spruce, at least three hundred years old, six metres in girth and nearly a hundred and seventy feet high. Photographs show it growing beside the Yakoun River with needles glowing a radiant gold in the sunlight. Sitka continue growing for around eight hundred years, so the Golden Spruce was still only a juvenile. It had special significance for the Haida and almost mythical status for visitors. In Haida legend the spruce was a boy who had been turned into a tree in a story that resembles the Greek tale of Orpheus leaving the underworld as well as the biblical tale of Lot's Wife. In the story, a Haida village is buried under deep snow that has fallen for months, perhaps as a punishment for some disrespectful act. The inhabitants die from starvation and exposure and the only survivors of this supernatural blizzard are an old man and a boy. They manage to dig themselves out of the drifts and leave their village stranded in permanent winter, knowing that they will never be able to go back. The old man warns the boy not to look behind him, but the boy can't resist the temptation to take one last look at the place where he had grown up and he is instantly turned into a tree. It appears to be a parable, rooted in the terrible consequences of the 'Great Dying', about the necessity to move on, looking forward, leaving behind the tragedies of the past. 'Don't look back!', it seems to say, or you'll be frozen in time.

The Golden Spruce Trail still exists, but I'm not going to follow it today because the legendary tree is no longer there. In 1997 it was illegally cut down by an unemployed logger called Grant Hadwin and is now only a rotting log on the riverbank. Hadwin claimed that he had cut down the Golden Spruce as a protest against the logging companies and their policy of 'clear-cut' logging and its environmental consequences. He was a former successful logger and road engineer who had become totally disillusioned with the industry and become an environmental activist. He had written a letter a few years earlier expressing the opinion that 'The Forest industry in British Columbia, appears to be one example, of economic remote controlled TERRORISM, on this planet, with professionals leading the way, in severe symptoms of denial, that there is any problem.'[79] Grant Hadwin was a loner, working by himself rather than with other groups, had a reputation as a bit of a hell-raiser, and had mental health issues. Friends considered him unstable. Opposition to the felling of old growth forests became an obsession.

On the night of January 20th 1997, Hadwin swam across the flooded Yakoun River with his chainsaw in a waterproof bag and spent several hours expertly cutting the tree and wedging it so that it would fall in the next high wind. He returned to Prince Rupert, publicly announced what he'd done, and a few days later the Golden Spruce fell, taking down surrounding trees with the force of an earthquake. What followed is one of the mysteries of Haida Gwaii. Hadwin was arrested and charged, but skipped bail before he could appear in court. A few months later his kayak and personal possessions were found on a remote island. No one knows whether he was murdered for his act of vandalism (there were many First Nation people who vowed to avenge the tree), had accidentally drowned in the sea while crossing the dangerous strait, or deliberately staged his own disappearance. No trace of him has ever been found.

But the Golden Spruce has had a surprising re-incarnation. Cuttings taken from the tree have been cultivated and re-planted. One of them grows in a protective cage in the Memorial Park in Port Clements and may one day, three hundred years from now, if climatic conditions allow, grow to the same size as its parent. But it will never have the same significance.[80]

It's a pleasure to drive the empty highway between green verges and the feathery walls of second growth pine forest. Almost too soon I can see the signs for the Tlell River and the Dodge's tyres rattle across the wooden bridge. I turn left towards the sea onto a narrow road, following the riverbank for about three kilometres until I see a blue No Enbridge sign and the name-board of Haida House. It turns out to be a cedarwood lodge with a drive-through porch that looks rather like a motel. I've been told that Haida House was a bear-hunting lodge in the days when it was acceptable to hunt bears with guns rather than cameras, but, inside the reception area, the pine walls are now hung with contemporary Haida art instead of stuffed trophies. I'm too early to check in, so I leave my luggage and decide to drive down to Skidegate for the rest of the afternoon.

The drive is magical. On my right, the forest draws back from the sea as the road skims the beach, around wide bays with endless views of the ocean. There are Haida Gwaii black-tailed deer grazing fearlessly on the green verges. I stop and get out to take photographs and am almost blown away by the fierce breeze off the sea. Back in the car the road curves around the edge of the land presenting view after view until a sign says 'Skidegate' and I'm descending gently into another bay with scattered houses below me and glimpses of distant mountainous islands offshore. I can feel my heart beating fast in anticipation.

One hundred and fifteen years ago, on Tuesday September 25th 1900, a young, idealistic anthropologist called John Swanton arrived in Skidegate by boat, having travelled from Victoria —

The Spirit in the Blood

quite by coincidence — with Charles Edenshaw. It was Swanton's
first visit to Haida Gwaii, and his initial reaction was one of
disappointment that so little of the Haida culture he had come to
study remained. '[In Skidegate] there is not an old house standing
— all have modern frame structures with the regulation windows
... The missionary has suppressed all the dances and has been
instrumental in having all the old houses destroyed — everything
in short that makes life worth living'.[81] Swanton was scathing
about the quality of the missionaries he met, writing to his
brother that 'It would honestly seem that the average west coast
divine were a man who cannot be endured elsewhere'. [82]

House poles in Skidegate at the end of the nineteenth century

Photographs show that only twenty years earlier, in 1881, the
shore at Skidegate was lined with about thirty 'bighouses' and
more than sixty carved totem and mortuary poles stood in front
of them. It was an impressive sight. By the time John Swanton
arrived, all the traditional houses and most of the poles had gone.
It was a scene of dereliction. Of the thousands of Haida who
had lived on the island, only a few hundred remained. Three
hundred of them were in Skidegate; the remnants of important

clans from the southern islands, isolated family survivors of 'The Great Dying', disconnected from their roots, separated from their children, forbidden to practise their own culture, demoralised, disorientated, bewildered, and fearful about what the future might hold. Life in Skidegate was, one writer has asserted, 'more like the Warsaw ghetto'.

John Swanton was not a typical product of North American colonial society. His father had died before he was born and he was brought up by his mother and grandmother. He was small in stature (an 'elf of a man'), shy, clever, interested from childhood in philosophy and psychology. He was a lifelong follower of the scientist and philosopher Emanuel Swedenborg. Swanton yearned for a more innocent time when 'students of nature were oftener content to observe her in the open than to carry her captive into a laboratory and put her through paces under "controlled" conditions'.[84] Context, Swanton believed, was important and he would have agreed with Thoreau's observation in *Walden* that 'it's not what you look at that matters; it's what you see'.

Swanton declined lodgings with the missionary and rented a small house near the fish oil factory where he could work undisturbed. He was there to write down as much of Haida poetry and mythology as he could, assisted by a translator, the son of a hereditary chief, who also instructed him in the unique Haida language, which was no mean feat of linguistics. 'The verb,' Swanton told Franz Boas, 'promises to be difficult.' Haida verbs, I've been told, are loaded with quite a lot of information and usually come at the end of the sentence, so they are tricky. But Swanton mastered them and many of the stories and poems are transcribed, verbatim, in the Haida language just as they were dictated to him by their owners. He was almost unique in this, because most anthropologists wrote down the stories they were told in their own languages, often summarising or Anglicising the plots.

One of the people Swanton worked with was a brilliant storyteller called Skaay in Haida, though referred to as John Sky in colonial records, considered by some to be 'the greatest Haida poet whose work survives'.[85] He came originally from the abandoned village of K'uuna, now known as Skedans. Swanton describes him as an old man 'who has a crippled back but is admitted on all hands to tell the old legends very correctly ... I consider him quite a find'.[86] It was Skaay who dictated the whole of the Raven story-cycle to Swanton, and Skaay was apparently the last person to remember the whole of it. *Raven Travelling* takes over an hour to tell and occupies several hundred pages in Swanton's notebook.

Raven Mask, Victoria Museum

It was this poem that first snagged my interest in Haida literature and mythology, not because of its historic content, but because what it said seemed to have direct contemporary relevance. At one point in the story Raven is invited under the sea for an audience with an old man. 'You are me,' he tells Raven, 'but you are that too', and he points to a group of young ravens preening themselves on top of one of the partitions in the house. The story seems to be establishing that all Nature is one. Raven is not only a bird, he is also human; he is both old and young at the same time, shape-shifting between the worlds of earth, sea and sky by means of a mental effort; 'He pushed his mind through/ and pulled his body after'.[87] There are no divisions that can't be transcended by the power of thought; ultimately we are all one.

At the beginning of the poem, in Skaay's telling, Raven discovers the first rock to emerge from the sea with spirit-beings sprawled across it like 'sea-cucumbers'. But in another version, told by Charles Edenshaw in Massett, Raven found the first humans in a clam shell on Rose Spit. In all variants of the story Raven is a discoverer, rather than a creator — an important difference from our own creation myths, but the long saga stresses his importance in the cosmos. Raven can swallow the sun, moon and stars which have been stolen by a greedy man and restore them to the heavens (Raven Steals Back the Light). But Raven is also himself a trickster and a thief, sexually voracious and permanently hungry. He commits every kind of excess and seems to exist as a metaphor for humankind in the world. Everything Raven does has consequences. His adventures show us ourselves, but they also show us how we stand in the scheme of the universe. There are wonderful characters, such as 'Voicehandler', who lives at the bottom of the sea, and 'Floodtide Woman' who is Raven's mother.

Swanton proved to be surprisingly enlightened. He recognised the importance of talking to Haida who had heard the stories as small children and who remembered them told by Elders who had learned the stories before they were altered and adapted by the influx of missionaries and exposed to European influences. Skaay, and others that Swanton listened to, had been born in the first half of the nineteenth century and had access to an active memory line going back a further hundred and fifty years through their parents and grandparents.

Swanton saw himself like Homer, 'on the shores of Ionia …collecting and arranging a literature already constructed … rescuing from oblivion the ancient lore of the North American Greeks'.[88] Swanton felt that what he was doing was so important he extended his original time in Haida Gwaii by several months; 'it would break my heart to feel there was a story left that I had failed to gather'. He was lonely and exhausted, often suffering from 'cabin fever', but he persisted. The more he transcribed the more he admired. 'The Haida pantheon was decorated just as lavishly as the Roman, and they seem even to have risen to the level of an Olympian Jove'.[89] Swanton was sad that he wasn't a musician and unable to take down the notation of the songs that were sung to him which he described as 'very sweet'.

His attitude to the Haida people was relatively unbiased for his time. He wrote in May 1901 '… It seems to me that the Indian is not … from a white standpoint, lying, cruel, immoral or thievish as the white man is. It seems to me rather that the qualities we often designate in this way are results deduced [in a perfectly logical manner]from his (ie the white man's) own super-conscious premise … which premise it has never occurred to him to question.'

But Swanton's bosses didn't hold the same opinions and the results of Swanton's efforts to preserve an oral literary tradition were largely ignored when he got back to New York. His gigantic achievement was hardly valued at all. Apart from a few publications, the bulk of his transcriptions languished in university archives for more than seventy years until contemporary scholars such as Robert Bringhurst began to study them and, eventually publish their translations. This was how I came to read them and, eventually, travel to Haida Gwaii.

As well as the myths themselves, the way the Haida structured their stories and poetry was a revelation for me. Oral literature has a logic of its own. The Haida transferred the form lines from their visual art to their literary art and it is rich in narrative lines. Where European-influenced poetry relies on rhyme, alliteration, rhythmic stresses and other word sound motifs, Haida poetry is structured by narrative elements. Robert Bringhurst calls this prosody '*noetic*', relating to the mind and the intellect.

'*Words and phrases are repeated; so therefore are their syntax and their sounds — and the sounds exhibit order, as sounds always do in meaningful speech. But the pattern in the foreground, and the pattern in control, is a pattern made of thought…. This is music of the mind more than music of the ear.*'[90]

Unfortunately this characteristic makes it difficult for people whose ears are trained to listen for word patterns, rather than complex narrative motifs. But it makes for forms that are just as valid as the Italian sonnet or the French rondelle or the Greek ode, and it's a way of structuring poetry that we don't seem to have tried on this side of the Atlantic. It makes me very excited to know that here, in Skidegate, I am at the very centre of this poetic tradition and the landscape that gave birth to it.

15. Skidegate

'Our culture is born of respect and intimacy with the land and sea and the air around us. Like the forest, the roots of our people are intertwined such that the greatest troubles cannot overcome us ...
Preamble to the Haida Constitution

If you come into Skidegate now, whether by boat or by road, as you round the point into the second bay, Kay Llnagaay, you will see a faint, but optimistic, echo of what was once there. A row of Bighouses stands along the shore with six totem poles in front and another standing alone on the edge of the sea. It's a sight that makes the breath catch in your throat and alters the rhythm of the heart.

This is the new Heritage Centre, built in 1970, which showcases the Haida way of life and some of its more important artefacts. It's one of the main things I've come to Skidegate to see.

The Bill Reid Centre, at Simon Fraser University, has a wonderful photograph of the original waterfront here, with a key to the images of each individual house and pole.[91] The houses had wonderful descriptive names such as the House to which the High Tide Comes, the Shining House, the House that Makes a Noise, House of the Stormy Sea, the Grizzly Bear House, the Thunder and Lightning House, House in which People Must Shout to be Heard, and — even more intriguing — the House Chiefs Peep at From a Distance. Each pole carried the crests and moieties of the clan members — a carved family history in front of each house. Taken together they told the stories that represented the history of the tribe. Bill Reid was telling the literal truth when he said that 'Totems are our history books'. You could tell at a glance who was related to who and what their status was. They are all long gone.

The Heritage Centre, Skidegate

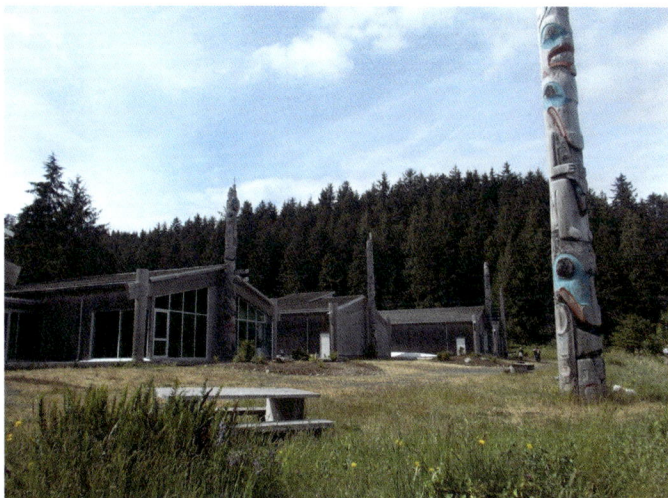

The recently erected Bighouses have more prosaic names; the Eating House, the Canoe Shed, and the Performing House. The museum section is called the Saving Things House. But they carry the spirit of the past and are very impressive. I tackle the Eating House first because it's a long time since I had breakfast and the coffee and cake at Pure Lake were consumed hours ago. The house is in traditional style, but has one glass wall that looks out across the bay to a cloud-wreathed island just offshore. The salmon chowder soup is wonderful with soda bread accompanied by a huge mug of coffee. I'm becoming a caffeine junkie here.

The bistro is almost empty but there's a woman sitting at one of the tables beside the window with a coffee mug beside her, obviously working. I recognise her photo from the internet as the owner of Haida House. She smiles at me in a friendly fashion, so I go over and introduce myself and ask whether it's possible to arrange any kind of tour down to Gwaii Haanas while I'm staying here. I'm desperate to visit the abandoned villages in the south, but because I'm so early in the season, I couldn't find a tour company on the internet who would accept a person travelling alone. They were only taking group bookings. Normally, in the tourist season, there are so many tours going there it's easy to slot someone in. If you have the money, you can make a personalised booking, hiring a float-plane or a boat for a private trip, but that's not an option for me. All the companies I contacted advised just taking pot-luck once I got here. Pot-luck it has to be and my current landlady just might know someone.

My luck, it seems, is very good indeed. "I'm going out there myself tomorrow with a couple of guests," she says. "I'll have to check with the guy who runs the boat, but I'm sure we can fit you in. Can I let you know tonight?"

I'm ecstatic.

The Saving Things House shelters a unique collection of artefacts salvaged from the lost villages of the south island, as well as Skidegate. There are tools and domestic objects as well as carvings, clothing and clan regalia. I find a *Taa Kaada* — a special type of knife used for splitting fish and scraping the soft interior of hemlock bark for food. It has a solid yew handle to fit into the palm of a hand, with a semi-circular steel blade embedded in it. There's also an early kind of adze used for carving. The handle is carved in the shape of a fish and the blade is formed from beaver teeth lashed to the wood with spruce fibres. The Haida must have been using tools like this long before they were able to obtain metal.

One room tells the story of the Haida Nation with images, films and soundtracks that recount the narrative of Haida Gwaii and the sad history of its colonisation and the attempts to obliterate its culture. They call the years between 1862 and the present day The Silent Years because of the 'loss of unfathomable amounts of knowledge, history and tradition' that died with the people during the Great Dying.

Among those losses is the knowledge of traditional medicine. The Haida had a diet that was extremely healthy. They ate a lot of fish, both fresh and dried, seal meat, whale meat, seaweed, wild fruit and berries. They also consumed quite a lot of Oolichan oil, which I suppose is the equivalent of our cod liver oil. The Oolichan is a small fish so rich in oil that it is called the 'Candle Fish', because once dried you can light it and it will burn like a torch. The coastal First Nation people used to net the Oolichan as it swarmed in millions into the rivers to breed at certain times of year. Some were dried, but others were fermented in a vat until their oil was released and could be stored. It was highly prized and the Haida traded some of their own specialities to get hold of it. They drank it at Potlatches, used it as a sauce for both fresh and dried fish during the winter, ladling it out of carved 'grease bowls' with ornate horn spoons. It's so rich that it's estimated that two spoonfuls of Oolichan oil is enough to keep an elderly person in calories and vitamins for almost a whole day.

Disruption of a culture by displacement, whether caused by war or natural disaster, also has an effect on diet and this is partly what happened to the Haida. It is an established fact that the health of a people, their culture, and environment are inextricably linked. The Great Dying, as well as the European style of life that First Nation people were expected to adopt, completely disrupted their rhythms of food collection and consumption. The felling of the forests took away sources of herbs and plant extracts they used for natural medicine. Many of the people who knew how to process these plants died. Due to pollution and commercial fishing the Oolichan fish vanished in many rivers and it became endangered. As a result of these disparate things, the health of the whole tribe suffered and it established a downward spiral of susceptibility to both local and imported diseases.

A recent scientific study has observed this happening throughout the twentieth century and into the twenty-first, wherever indigenous cultures have collided with colonisers. The authors state that: 'it is hard to overstate just how quickly knowledge [of natural, nutritional medicine] can be lost after a tribe makes contact with the outside world. Once extinguished, this knowledge, along with the tribe's self-sufficiency, can never fully be reclaimed. Historically, what has followed the loss of endemic health systems in many indigenous groups is near total dependency on the rudimentary and extremely limited external health care that is available in such remote and difficult-to-access locations. Not surprisingly, in most countries, indigenous groups have the highest rates of mortality and disease.'[92]

The Constitution of the Haida Nation, formulated in 1974 when the Council of the Haida Nation was formed, is on the wall of the Heritage Centre to read. It affirms the Haida commitment to the preservation of the environment and the importance of standing together in order to protect their survival. There's a quote from Chief Skidegate; 'Just as one tree standing alone would soon be destroyed by the first strong wind which came along, so it is impossible for any person, any family, or any country to stand against the troubles of this world.'[93] Everything is connected; we have to work together.

The Haida principle of respect for the living world is prominently displayed. It is a Haida imperative that, when food-gathering, you have to give thanks for the animal or plant that has given its life to feed you. 'The first salmon of the year goes back to feed the river. And some is given back for others to share in, like the eagles.' This recognises the need to treat the whole ecology with respect, because we are part of it and need its resources. The Haida believe that the environment is not there to be plundered for commercial profit, and they must only take what they need 'so as to not deplete any area of its riches'. The Haida Constitution also stresses the need to pass down these values and traditions from parent to child. 'The living generation accepts the responsibility to ensure that our heritage is passed on to the following generations. On these islands our ancestors lived and died and here too we will make our homes until called away to join them in the great beyond.'[94] The Haida philosophy seems to encapsulate everything that the modern world needs to hear.

I meet Julia and Colette and their sons on my way round. We all seem to be on the same quest and fated to bump into each other at regular intervals. Today they are being given a guided tour of the museum and a special demonstration of Haida weaving. There are some lovely examples of this on display. The

Haida used to make all their clothes out of animal skins, furs and natural fibres. They used the roots of spruce trees to weave baskets and hats and other domestic objects. They also used cedar bark to make garments and blankets. There was a special technique for harvesting the bark so that the tree wasn't harmed. Just one strip would be cut out, then soaked, stripped and pounded into fibres which could then be woven into soft, pliable skirts and cloaks which were incredibly durable. They were also very pretty. One of the most desirable garments was a Chilcat blanket — a ceremonial cloak made out of the creamy fleece of a type of mountain goat

Button Blanket with Eagle motif

179

found on the mainland, woven together with cedar fibres. The blankets were woven with complex designs illustrating the stories of the clan, coloured with natural dye in yellow, black and blue. They had long cream fringes and were sometimes trimmed with fur. Haida objects were traded to obtain the goat fleeces and these cloaks were high status objects. Today, the Haida wear blankets made of contemporary woollen fibres, in vivid red and black, with appliqued motifs to declare their clan moiety, decorated with mother of pearl buttons in traditional patterns. Some of these are on display too.

In the main room are three house poles, rescued from their original locations and preserved as examples of a high period in Haida art. The ceilings are too low to have the poles at their full height, so they are displayed in sections. But this doesn't detract from their beauty. Some of them are very wide in diameter, giving some indication of the size of the original, old-growth, trees they were carved from. The one that gripped me most strongly was the pole taken from the Shadow House at T'aanu. It celebrates the Eagle clan and has a carved eagle with the face of an ancestor carved into its tail. There's a horned owl in the process of transforming into a human being and at the bottom a killer whale and a grizzly bear. At the top of the pole sit the three watchmen, with their tall hats, looking in three different directions, representing earth, sea and sky.

The Haida poles in the museum have a power and dignity far exceeding any other First Nation carved poles I've seen so far. They affect you emotionally at a very deep level. I find myself holding my breath as I stand in front of them. This is something that only happens with art, particularly great art. It has the power of communicating something even if you don't understand the subject matter. You can feel it. Emily Carr described this quality as 'Strong thought' on the part of the original carver.

Outside, with a mug of tea in my hand, I sit on the grass among the wildflowers that fringe the waterfront looking out over the sea, with the Heritage Centre rising behind me like a wooden cliff. There's a gigantic totem pole to my right (the bottom part of it is old, from T'aanu apparently, with a newly carved upper section) and — if I don't look round — I can imagine that the old Bighouses, house poles and mortuary poles of the original village are still there. There are two islands in front of me in the bay and tall grasses growing up on the shore with dandelions and clover as well as ferns and small alders. The sun is beating on my back and there's a strong, herbal smell in the air mixing with the ozone from the sea.

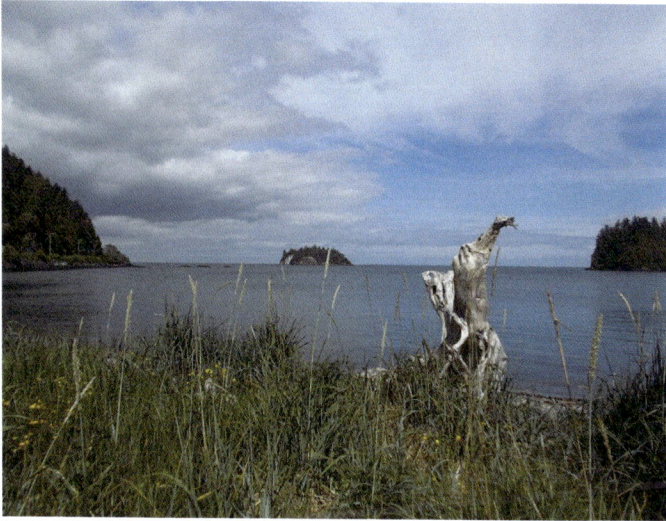

Skidegate. The bay and islands from the Heritage Centre

Behind me are the six new poles that represent six of the abandoned Haida villages; Skedans, Skidegate, Chaatl, Cumshewa, T'aanu and Ninstints. They were carved by Guujaaw, James 'Jim' Hart, Robert Davidson and other eminent Haida artists. In the carving shed a new pole is being carved, as well as a canoe, by one of Guujaaw's sons and his apprentices. There's another canoe which has been lifted outside for a group of people to inspect. It has a beautiful painted prow and stern in vivid colours of black and red and yellow and blue. This is Lootaas — Bill Reid's famous 'Wave-eater', the fifteen metre canoe that took his body on its last journey to T'aanu, carved, like all the Haida canoes, from a single tree trunk. A guide explains to me that suitable trees for canoes, weighing several tons, were often found too far inland to carry down to the sea, so they would be felled and hollowed out in situ before being dragged to the nearest launching point.

The speed and nimble handling of the Haida war canoes — some of them ninety feet long — surprised the British. They could easily outpace and outmanoeuvre the British naval ships. With their carved and painted prows they were also very beautiful — an awesome sight for their adversaries. For longer journeys, rather than coastal hops, they were fitted with outriggers and sails. In 1874, the Reverend Collison — a missionary at Skidegate — recalled seeing a fleet of Haida canoes approaching. 'It consisted of some forty large canoes, each with two snow white sails spread, one on either side of each canoe, which caused them to appear like immense birds or butterflies, with white wings outspread, flying shorewards.'[95]

These canoes were capable of covering tremendous distances. In the first decade of the twentieth century, to prove the point, two men set out from Victoria on an epic journey in a dugout canoe called the Tilikum. One of the men disembarked at Fiji, after a disagreement at gun point, but the other, Captain John Voss, sailed the Tilikum across the Pacific to New Zealand, surviving several shipwrecks (and controversy around the death of another companion), before paddling the canoe back round Cape Horn and across the Atlantic to Europe. The Tilikum ended its life in the mud of the Thames estuary in London in 1904, where it would have rotted and disappeared forever if a fund hadn't been raised for its repatriation and preservation in 1929. It's now in the Maritime Museum in Victoria, where — if I'd known about it — I could have seen it when I was there.

The sun is beginning to disappear over the hills, on a long and very active day. It's time to drive back to Tlaall and Haida House. The ocean view highway looks beautiful in the evening light. The tide is beginning to come in and the waves are smashing up on the rocks in clouds of spray. There are deer and eagles and hardly any cars at all.

Haida House is completely constructed of wood inside and out which gives it a strange, rustic feel, like a log cabin; but it's huge. I'm taken upstairs and there's a long corridor with rooms

Balance Rock, Skidegate

going off on both sides. I have one facing the river. It's big, with two single beds and a chest of drawers orphaned against one wall. There's an ensuite and a carpet on the floor, but it all feels rather spartan. Despite the original Haida art on the walls, I'm afraid the bear-hunting lodge will take a long time to exorcise.

Downstairs there's a bar, opening out onto the river, and a room they call 'the den', which has a fridge and a microwave and a kettle. Visitors are requested not to cook meals. The best wifi is here, but isn't very good. I've got used to this already on Haida Gwaii. It's not a place for internet junkies. Or mobile phone addicts. There's a signal here and another in Skidegate or Masset, but you can forget it anywhere else. I'm not missing instant communication. In fact it's a relief to be cut off for a while from our so-called advanced technology.

I go and get a glass of wine from the bar and find a place in the dining room, which closes after 8.30. Everyone eats early here and I'm already quite late. The staff are all Haida. The girl who takes my order has a braided Haida headband, trimmed with fur. The menu is mouth-watering and apparently they have a French chef. It looks as if the restaurant is one very good reason to stay here, but the prices are eyebrow raising. When I think about it, I realise that everything is being trucked over from the mainland, or air-freighted, so their overheads must be enormous. There's a party of young Americans at a nearby table getting drunk on wine and beer and they are very loud. I wonder if this is going to be a good experience and I'm hoping that they aren't the people that my hostess is taking to Skedans tomorrow. But it turns out that they've been on an adventure holiday and tonight is their last night.

There's a message when I go up to bed that I need to be at the jetty in Queen Charlotte by 7.30am tomorrow. I can hardly sleep for excitement.

16. The Great Dying

The birds are silent in the woods.
Just wait: Soon enough
You will be quiet too.
Robert Hass

I'm awake at 5am listening to the voice of the forest. There are ravens and a couple of bald eagles and the musical bell-notes of other, smaller birds I can't identify. There's one bird I think of as the 'telephone bird', which has a distinctive call like a mobile phone ring-tone. If this was England, so close to the sea, the early morning air would be raucous with seagulls, but here the noisy flocks that mark out our coasts are absent. There are two dominant birds — raven and eagle — both at home in the forest and the sea, nesting in one and feeding on the other. That's what this place is about — the conversation between the forest and the sea. The Haida have always lived on the fragile margin between them. Like eagle and raven, their prosperity came from their ability to live off the resources that forest and ocean offered in terms of food, clothing and shelter. And they were so prosperous and well-fed that they had time to devote to developing their art and poetry. It's only secure cultures that can afford to designate individuals as artists.

As soon as I've had an early breakfast I have to get in the car and drive down to the quayside at Queen Charlotte. This is the first time I've been there and I'd expected a small town, but it's the size of a village and very European. There's a big new hospital being built, a tourist information centre, shops, a ferry port and lots of fishing jetties. I find the jetty I've been directed

185

to without much trouble and park the Dodge on a grass verge. I'm going out in a Zodiac with four other guests, all middle-aged Canadians, accompanied by my Haida House hostess, her friend Jags (owner of the Beanstalk), a Haida artist called Patrick from Tlell, and three Haida crew. We're kitted out as if for an arctic fishing trawler. I have insulated oilskin overalls, a huge ocean-going buoyancy jacket, and deck boots three sizes too big. Add to that sunglasses to protect my eyes from the wind, a woolly hat and gloves and I look as if I'm going to Alaska! But, steering out of Skidegate Bay, into the wild and treacherous Hecate Strait, I can see that they are needed. The wind is behind us and the Zodiac slams from swell to swell, powering south along the dark, forested coastline of Moresby Island, the mountains growing higher and higher the further south we go. After a couple of hours your fingers freeze on the grab rail and the wind makes the bones of your face ache. Spray decorates your oilskins with salt and fogs up the sunglasses.

Hecate Strait, in the Zodiac

The day is overcast, but once again there are rumours of orca in the area. The boat's skipper, Dan, says he's keeping an eye open for them, but there's very little wildlife in evidence. We spot a shearwater, and a couple of shags closer to shore. Dan makes a detour to small rocky islands surrounded by kelp where there are colonies of sea lions — favourite food for orca and once in danger of extinction. They bob up warily to watch us as we drift past. Fishermen used to be paid for every seal nose they brought in, until they were declared a protected species. But apparently sea lion numbers have been increasing recently and it's possible that the hunting ban on them will be lifted to allow a small number to be seasonally killed, in line with Haida tradition. They live and feed among the kelp beds which used to be extensive around the islands. One of the other traditional Haida foods is the herring eggs that stick to the kelp and which are prized as a delicacy once they are dried.

Dan points out Lyell Island — a dark, tree-covered hummock rising up out of the grey sea — and talks about the protests that saved, not only Lyell, but much of the larger Moresby Island from commercial logging. Shortly after the successful defence orchestrated by Guujaaw, the Gwaii Haanas National Park Reserve was created here in 1987, as a protected environment. The green, forested shores we can see further south are part of it. One of the other passengers asks about the forest covering the hillsides, which looks ragged, untidy, sprinkled with the white trunks of dead trees. Dan explains that this is old-growth which, unlike planted forest, has no uniformity. It's a mixture of new and mature trees as well as those that have died and are waiting to be felled to the forest floor by winter winds. There, they will rot and become 'nurse logs', providing nutrition for seedlings which may take root and grow from their carcasses. The ragged appearance is partly a result of the varying ages of individual trees and partly to do with the diversity of species — which includes red cedar, yellow cedar, hemlock and sitka spruce, among others. Wild, old-growth forest is untidy.

Just as I'm beginning to get very cold and stiff, the pitch of the boat's engine slows and we begin to turn towards an inlet. This, Dan tells us, is Skedans, known to the Haida as K'uuna. It's the village where the storyteller Skaay was born, and Jags tells us that his family also belongs here. His father was a hereditary chief.

A young boy who is crewing the boat also belongs to the Eagle moiety of K'uuna, though he and his parents were born and have lived all their lives in Skidegate.

Dan takes the Zodiac into a small bay as close to the steep, sloping, shingle beach as he can safely do. There's an aluminium ladder and a member of the crew to help us all down into the shallows. Sea legs are surprisingly wobbly on the slippery pebbles. Ravens are circling overhead.

"Watch out for those ravens," Dan says, with a big grin. "They'll steal anything they can get. They're rotten!"

The ravens have realised that the arrival of a boat signifies an opportunity for entertainment. They're partial to people's lunches, their flash drives and camera lens covers; anything small enough to lift. While we sit on the driftwood peeling off our waterproof layers, the ravens keep an opportunistic eye on us from the other end of the beach.

The beach, Skedans K'uuna

Coffee is produced from big flasks and two young girls come out of the trees to greet us. Skiil and her friend Leanne are 'Watchgirls'. Because no one lives in Gwaii Haanas, the ancient villages are unprotected from tourist vandalism and theft. Precious poles have been cut down and loaded onto visiting yachts and other artefacts, even human remains, have been stolen. So volunteers of all age groups take it in turns to spend a couple of weeks living in a log house at each of the historic locations, acting as guardians for their cultural heritage. They have photovoltaic plates to provide enough electricity for a fridge and a computer. They have radio communication, compost toilets and their own boat. Usually they have pure spring water to drink, cook and wash but, since the drought began, the springs in Gwaii Haanas have dried up. Dan has brought plastic containers of drinking water over on the Zodiac.

The village of Skedans/K'uuna was built on a spit of land with a bay on each side of it and a steep rocky cliff behind. This was a good defensive position, offering escape from attack, but also alternative launching beaches for canoes whatever the direction of the wind. Once, the bay would have been lined with Bighouses with their poles in front; now it is fringed with trees, but sheltered under the trees are the ruins of the community.

While the others are drinking their coffee, I slip away inland to get my first glimpses of it by myself. Emily Carr described sitting on the shore at the edge of the forest canopy listening to the sea playing 'a game of toss' with the trees and her image is very exact. The wind in the branches above me sounds like an echo of the surf swishing backwards and forwards over the shingle. Among the trunks of new growth firs, the rotting remains of carved poles lean away from the wind. Their deeply cut images, punctuated by the drilled holes of woodpeckers, are blurred by the erosion of rain and storm. The teeth and paws of a beaver, the wing of a raven, are still discernible, but after more than a hundred years of exposure to the elements, the wood is splitting and crumbling. Some poles are already lying on the ground, covered in moss, busy returning to the earth they grew out of as saplings hundreds of years before. I've been told that in twenty years not a single pole will remain. In my lifetime they will cease to exist. On the ground, square, deep pits, criss-crossed by moss-covered fallen beams, mark the sites of the Bighouses. I close my eyes and try to imagine what it would have been like to live here.

Raven house pole

K'uuna was a permanent winter village. During spring, summer and autumn the Haida moved around to take advantage of seasonal crops; the salmon runs, the halibut fishing, kelp harvesting, cranberry picking. Each food had its moment on the calendar and its own location. Richer families had houses in each place, the poorer families just erected corner posts and then stripped out the cedar planks that formed the walls and ceilings and took them with them, towed behind their canoes like rafts. But winter storms in Hecate Strait were no place for a canoe and winter was a time to light fires, stay in one place, tell stories, hold Potlatches, dance and sing. The Haida had no calendars and no clocks; one Elder, when asked how they knew when it was time to move, answered, "The moon tells us".

Everyone is moving inland now, the party led by the Watchgirls, Jags and two members of the crew. We're shown the compost toilet and two of the boys start to light a fire to cook our lunch. While we wait for it to kindle, Jags takes us on a tour of the village. His father, a hereditary chief here, used to bring Jags for camping trips to Skedans when he was a boy and tell him stories about what it was like to grow up here before the village was abandoned. The young children would be running around naked, rubbed in bear grease to protect against the cold and then in wood ash to screen out the sun. Apparently the missionaries were disgusted. But the bear grease protected children from the cold water and heavy, european style clothes often drowned people when they fell in, because of the weight of water they soaked up.

He shows us the chief's house — now only a green, moss-covered pit criss-crossed with fallen beams. It had been a six beam house, dug down into the earth, three tiers deep and would have been about forty feet from the base of the house pit to the highest roof beam. It was called 'The Sound of Clouds Rowing Across the Sky' and could accommodate several hundred people for a potlatch. He also takes us on a tour of the poles and talks about the stories that they tell — stories handed on to him by his father. The rings at the top of the pole, or on the watchmen's hats, are there to state how many potlatches a particular individual has given. One of the poles here has ten rings, indicating a rich and successful chief.

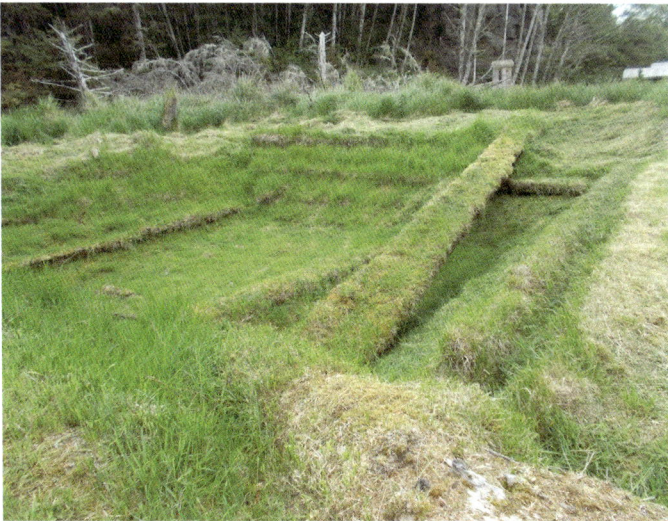

"The Sound of Clouds Rowing Across the Sky"

Jags also explains the way secondary growth takes root in the stumps of the old corner posts of the houses, the new saplings using the rotting wood as a nursery. Carvings are still visible on some of the poles lying horizontal on the ground. The young crewman from Skedans, who is of the Eagle moiety, also has the Sculpin as one of his emblems and he shows us a fallen pole with the Sculpin — an ugly deepwater fish — carved on the underside where it's been protected from the weather. It is probably the pole that marked the house his ancestors lived in. Not all the poles can be deciphered. An intricately carved Raven on one of the standing poles has been reduced only to wings and tail and is in imminent danger of collapse. It looks so frail that Jags speculates it might not survive this year's winter storms.

While we are standing beside the house pit, looking at the poles, a black-tailed deer emerges from the forest and walks through the glade between us, quite unafraid. I could have put out my hand and touched it.

Lunch is salmon and duck grilled over the open fire with salad, made by Dan, and some cake for pudding. It's all delicious. Afterwards they teach us a Haida welcome song and then Jags talks about his visits to Skedans throughout his life, the camping trips first with his father and then alone. The stories become more sombre. So many people died here in the smallpox epidemics of the 1860s that there was no one to bury the dead. The Black Death in Europe killed only about 30% of the population; here the death rate was around 90%. Skidegate was also hit hard, though it was never abandoned. The Reverend Collison, the first missionary to arrive there, talked about the horror of the Bighouses that had become charnel houses for the dead, packed so full of bodies that the stench was almost unbearable. He described how weather damaged the woodwork and animals made holes and dragged away the bones, scattering them over the ground. Collison couldn't understand how the people of Skidegate could live with it. But, as survivors of a tragedy as enormous as this, they were afflicted with a kind of hopelessness in the face of death. They had left behind their own unburied dead in their villages and may well have expected to die themselves. I've read about it all in books, but here, in one of the places where it happened, hearing the story told by someone whose grandparents were among the dispossessed, his wider family among the dead, it has an additional power.

Jags tells us that there was also evidence that the sickness was deliberately spread. In 1863 a sick elderly man was put ashore at a healthy village, by a crew under a Captain called Francis Poole, who knew the consequences. Everyone subsequently died. There were stories of infected blankets being put into canoes. The result was horrific. Jags talks of babies being found alive still trying to suckle from their dead mothers; old people unable to hunt or feed themselves, who died from starvation when their children died. When he came here with his father as a child, the ground was littered with the bones of the unburied dead. Whenever they found human remains, they covered them up out of respect. Jags says that it's still possible to stumble across them today.

Of thirty thousand people, eventually only about five hundred were left — many of them women. Susan Williams, Guujaaw's great-grandmother, was born in the 1850s and was one of the last of the old people to leave Skedans. She was already old when she canoed into Skidegate with all her possessions, but she lived to be over a hundred. Women like Susan Williams were able to pass on their knowledge and their stories to a younger generation eager to re-possess their lost culture. It is a tribute to Victorian patriarchy that John Swanton did not interview a single female storyteller. You have to wonder how much richer his 'word-hoard' would have been if the women had been asked to tell him what they knew.

Things hidden when the villages were abandoned are still being discovered. Once, when Jags was exploring some caves in the cliffs above the village, he found a collection of cedar boxes, containing regalia, stacked up at the back, just as they had been left, and there was a Shaman's sceptre in a crack in the roof of the cave. When he got back to Skidegate, Jags told the Chief about them and was given permission to bring them back to put in the museum for protection. Looting has been a big problem. Before Moresby Island became a protected environment loggers sometimes dragged huge trees through the forest and obliterated houses and poles. You can still see where that has happened at Skedans. And loggers often had the perfect opportunity to loot the treasures that had been left behind. One logger's cabin, after a tip off, was found to be full of Haida artefacts that he was intending to sell once he got back to the mainland.

Tourists on boats have been a big problem too. The owners of a yacht moored at Prince Rupert were discovered to have part of a totem pole hidden on the deck under a tarpaulin. It was the famous Flood Pole from K'uuna, now in the museum. Jags tells us the story of how Raven had an argument with Chief Kingii of K'uuna and in a fit of anger caused a big flood. But Kingii also had supernatural powers and he made his 'potlatch hat' grow more and more rings, higher and higher, and the villagers were able to climb up the hat and escape drowning. The mountain behind the village is still called Kingii. The story seems to describe a Tsunami, of which there have been many in the past. Like Noah and the Flood, the story has its roots in history, but also has contemporary relevance. Dan says he went camping with a friend a few months ago on the west coast and going into the forest to find a sheltered place, they found a tidemark of debris, plastic water bottles, driftwood and seaweed, more than sixty feet from the high tide mark. It's no wonder that most of the Haida settlements were on the more sheltered, eastern side of the islands.

I talk to one of the Watchgirls, Skiil, about how it feels to stay here. She says it's hard to come to terms with what she calls 'the powerful energy' of the site, but that she and her friend love the place and the opportunity to learn about their people and their stories. As we walk along the path back to the beach with the boat crew it's good listening to them talking to each other about their lineages, and discussing with each other the correct version of a story, or the right way to pronounce a word. All these young people are re-learning what it means to be Haida.

Skiil is arguing with one of the boys about Emily Carr — he disapproves of her, says her art is crap, but that because she's European, she's become nationally famous, whereas Haida art, which is so much better, isn't valued because it's indigenous.

"Emily," he says, "was just copying and it was useless."

But the girl defends Emily — says she was a woman doing a very special thing for women at the time and being put down because she was a woman.

As we walk back, Jags stops beside one of the poles and points out the, now faint, carving of a killer whale. It represents one of the K'uuna stories about a Haida princess who went down to the edge of the water to wash out an otter's skin that she was curing. While she crouched on the beach she was taken by a killer whale. Her husband loved her so much he went down into the sea to get her back.

Dressed once more in our bulky oilskins and loaded, like space walkers, back into the Zodiac, Dan tells us that we're to get an additional treat. Patrick, the Haida artist from Tlell, is from Cumshewa, a village further up the coast. His father was hereditary chief there, but Patrick hasn't been back in ten years. Dan thinks that we can make a stop at Cumshewa. You have to go in on a rising tide because of the shallowness of the inlet, but the tide should be just right for us today.

Cumshewa Inlet

The bay is wider at Cumshewa and the land slopes more gently. Dan beaches the Zodiac in shallow water and we paddle up onto the shore. Because there's no rocky cliff behind this village, there's more of a sense of the forest coming right down to the sea. Emily Carr spent a lot of time in her journal trying to explain the pull of the forest. It is very dark and very secret. You feel it has things to tell and yet it is also a place to experience fear. There is, in the green darkness, a silence that draws you in. At first you hear nothing, then small perturbations of the air, a snowfall of pine needles and the exhalations of moss. A twig cracks under a deer's hoof and the wind, lifting off the sea, ruffles the shaggy crests of the cedars.

The group go off with Patrick to look at the lodge his parents erected there and where he spent a lot of time during his childhood. I go off on my own to explore the secret heart of the forest. Further in, past the abandoned, moss-covered house-pits, there are the ruins of great trees. Several have been felled in a storm, leaving a clearing piled high with branches and splintered wood. I sit down on one of the broken limbs — itself bigger than most tree trunks I've seen in Europe — and listen. My own heartbeat, like a footfall, fills the space between the branches and the forest floor, every nerve of me alive, and every cell aware. Millions of trees have died and dropped and crumbled into terracotta dust here since the end of the ice age. I breathe it in, every breath sounding louder than the one before. It is the only human sound I can hear. It's very peaceful under the trees and it comforts me to think that all chaos and misery in the end come to this, what Marlowe called 'a green thought in a green shade'. The dead sleep very quietly at Cumshewa.

When I come back to the boat, the others are still wandering around in the next bay, so I sit on a log on the beach talking to Dan. He tells me he's an activist against Enbridge. A couple of years ago he and a group of other First Nation people decided to go to the Enbridge AGM in Toronto to find out what was going on and to lobby against the pipeline. But they were instantly recognised as First Nation. They were surrounded by security and evicted as soon as they tried to go through the door. But one of their PAs was Chinese and she was allowed in without any questions at all and was able to report back. Dan managed to talk to one of the Enbridge board directors, door-stepping her in a hotel lobby. She asked him, "Why are you trying to bite the hand that feeds you?" There was no recognition at all of the fact that there might be environmental concerns that needed to be considered before the project was approved. "It's not about money," Dan says.

On the train back to Vancouver, Dan recognised a couple of Royal Canadian Mounted police from Massett in plain clothes. This was not a coincidence, the police had been shadowing the group since they left home. He tells me that this is a normal government tactic. But Dan is actually quite positive about the future — he thinks they will win, that they will be able to delay the project until solar power and renewables become cheap enough to overtake fossil fuel. Dan is very passionate about it all — once more Haida Gwaii is at the forefront of the clash between capitalism and the welfare of ordinary human beings. And this time they have highly trained lawyers, whose skills have been honed in the fight for their land rights.

Where we're sitting, there's an island just offshore with a pebble causeway that was just walkable when we arrived, but is now disappearing under the incoming tide.

"That's Mortuary Island," Dan tells me, and explains that there are still human bones lying around on it. Apparently the numbers of dead were so great here — often hundreds at a time — that the stench was too great to bear and boats coming into shore turned back. The dead remained unburied here too.

The return journey back is less pleasant than the trip out. The weather has changed while we were at Cumshewa. Out in the Hecate Strait again there's a flood tide coming towards us with huge swells building up against the strong southwesterly wind at our backs. Dan warns us that it's going to be 'lively', shouting over the racket of the outboards and the wind tearing at our flotation jackets, but he also explains that he used to be a coastguard and has been out in more turbulent seas than this. We're doing more than twenty knots, swinging around to meet the swells in the best

Mortuary Island, Cumshewa

possible way, then swinging back onto the navigation line as they pass. It's like a white knuckle fairground ride and some of the other passengers have faces the same colour as the ocean. But, although I'm soaked with sea spray, I feel more exhilarated than afraid.

Most of the wildlife seems to have vanished with the weather. There are only the little black and white birds they call Ancient Murrelets that lift out of the water in panic as we pass, skimming the surface like flying fish before disappearing into it again. It's a member of the Auk family and Dan tells us that half the world's population breeds here. They wait, just off shore, for night to fall so that they can return to their burrows on the cliff-tops in the safety of darkness. The way they appear up out of the water is like a magic trick.

The boat slows almost to a standstill. Dan explains that we now have to cross the main current to get over the bar into Skidegate inlet. We are 'turning left' across the Hecate Strait against the flood tide. At one point he jokes about having to go to Prince Rupert instead. The way Dan zig-zags to and fro, finding a path through the turbulent mass of water, is impressive. Suddenly, the wind eases, the motion of the Zodiac subsides and we're in the calmer waters of the bay, safely back to harbour. As I climb out of the boat onto the jetty, I feel slightly giddy and my cheeks are burning with the salt wind. We ditch the oilskins and share a hug. There's a feeling of having been through a very special experience.

Back at Haida House I'm so tired I can barely keep my eyes open. Time for a carton of instant porridge heated in the microwave, some fresh fruit and biscuits, a mug of hot tea, then a shower and the blissful falling into bed.

17. Encounter With a Bear

'If you go down to the woods today
You'd better not go alone'.
Lyric by Jimmy Kennedy, 1932.

I'm having a couple of lazy days, sitting on remote beaches watching the sea, walking in the woods, drinking coffee in Jags Beanstalk (where I found Guujaaw having coffee with Dan), and revisiting the Heritage Centre just in case there's something I've missed. I can't get enough of the carvings, particularly the ones from T'aanu.

Sunday was a difficult day — everything seemed to be closed and it was too wet to walk far (welcome rain for Haida Gwaii). It was the kind of rain you get in Scotland, persistent and soaking, yet not very heavy when you're out in it. The landscape even looked Scottish; misty hills across the inlet and the occasional ray of sun breaking through on the water. After a short, damp walk in the woods, I had fish and chips in Queen Charlotte and did some souvenir hunting for presents for my family in the one or two shops that were still open.

In Skidegate they have what in the north of England we used to call 'parlour shops'. They open up a part of their house as a shop to sell a small quantity of things, often made by themselves or members of their family. Skidegate seems much more prosperous than Old Massett. I get the impression that the Haida here are much more in control, owning the businesses whole or in part. And there's probably more work here — logging, the ferry port to the mainland and to Sandspit, and as a consequence more hotels and businesses to service the tourist trade. Skidegate is so much nearer to Gwaii Haanas.

In the little shops there's beautiful hand-carved jewellery on sale, screen-printed Haida designs, carved wooden objects, as well as masks and miniature chests. I can't buy much because, although my luggage allowance from Vancouver to England is enormous, the limit on the small turboprop I'm flying out of Masset on is very small — little more than hand luggage. For myself I buy a screen printed Raven scarf designed by Jim Hart in a dramatic red and black that I like very much. It's a small indulgence to join the clam shell and the pebbles and the raven feathers I've gathered from the beaches and the forest floor. My pockets are full of beach-combings.

Last night I had dinner with Julia and Colette and their sons. They had chartered a float plane to take them to Ninstints, a world heritage site on an island at the southern tip of Gwaii Haanas, one of the wonders of Haida Gwaii, where a large number of carved poles still stand on the edge of the sea. I am very envious, but float plane hire is way beyond my allowance and I'm too early in the season to find a group I can be squeezed into.

Julia described how their pilot had taken them out looking for whales and they were lucky enough to find a group of humpbacks feeding. They were using their characteristic method of circling the prey and sending up a net of bubbles to trap the fish, then surfacing in the middle of it with their mouths open. It sounded spectacular. We had a lovely evening sharing our experiences of Haida Gwaii and I now have two invitations to stay when I go back to Vancouver. Julia, Colette and Chris are going back tomorrow, but Ben is staying on because he finds it so magical. Jags Beanstalk doesn't have any spare rooms so he's moving up to Haida House.

This evening, my last evening, I've decided to walk up the beach to where the Tlell River pours out into the sea. It's low tide, so I wonder if I might be able to wade out across it to where the wreck of the ship Pesuta sits further up the beach. I'm taking sandwiches with me because the dining room at Haida House is closed tonight.

Broom growing in the sand dunes

One of the best things about Haida House is its closeness to the sea. I walk out of the door, through sand dunes covered in wildflowers and out onto the beach. The yellow broom is beginning to flower and fill the air with perfume. There are blueish purple flowers that seem to belong to the pea family and white stars on slender stems I can't identify. Under the shelter of the silvery blue marram grass, wild strawberries are beginning to ripen. As I walk along the edge of the water, a sea lion pops its head above the surface and watches me for a while before up-flippering and swimming away. An eagle is circling overhead, giving me the once-over and a tiny sand pipit hops along beside me, but at a safe distance. It's as if nature is sending guardians to watch me — idiotic, I know, but one is in myth territory here. Imagination, but comforting.

I'm feeling depressed because I only have a couple of days left on Haida Gwaii and I still haven't solved my own personal dilemma. For the past three years I've been trying to live in two places on opposite sides of Europe, commuting between them and finding it increasingly difficult to work with the constant disruption of moving from place to place. The small rented house in Italy doesn't feel like home and I can't write easily there away from my books and my personal possessions. I miss my children, my family. But my partner needs to be there for his work. If I go back permanently to my home in England again it means sustaining a long distance relationship, just at a time in life when you most need companionship. What am I going to do? Where to live? How to live? It seems impossible for my partner to work in England, but equally impossible for me to uproot myself entirely and put down roots again in a foreign country. I'm constantly homesick. The Irish poet Patrick Kavanagh called this need to belong 'The Great Hunger'. I've lived for extensive periods as an expatriate in Africa and the Middle East, but always with the knowledge that there was a home to come home to, to re-charge the creative batteries, in my beloved Cumbria, the northern powerhouse of the imagination. It is to me what Haida Gwaii is to the Haida.

The New Zealand writer Janet Frame wrote in an essay that all writers are, in essence, exiles. 'All writers are exiles wherever they live … and their work is a lifelong journey towards the lost land.'[96] Perhaps this is because, as writers, we have to stand outside our own experience and look at it objectively in order to write about it. We're always trying to get back to the 'lost land' — those moments experienced and gone — at the core of our imaginative lives. The writer Edward Said — born in Palestine and an exile since 1947 — wrote that what we do as writers is 'by necessity', to make ourselves 'a house of words' to dwell in.[97] It's an interesting notion. We are all 'writing ourselves back home', wherever home is.

A lot of writers appear to thrive in exile. Katherine Mansfield, whose biography I wrote, spent her life outside New Zealand, writing brilliant evocations of her homeland. But she felt that her stories were only shadows of what she could have achieved if she'd been able to return. 'Really, I am sure it does a writer no good to be transplanted — it does harm. One reaps the glittering top of the field, but there are no sheaves to bind.'[98] This is how I feel too, when separated from the sturdy taproot I've been putting down in the Lake District fells since I was born. Perhaps it takes three generations before you can take root and know where you belong?

I've realised, while being here in Haida Gwaii, the importance of roots — they nourish and sustain. For some belonging may not be important, there are many people who are content to be nomads, but for me, however much I love to travel, it is essential to be based in 'one dear perpetual place'. That, at least, is now clear. Maintaining a relationship across a continent is not easy, but that is what I'm going to have to do. So, I suppose a decision of sorts has been made.

Life has to be lived to the full — not left in a drawer like a gift too precious to be used. But, unless you are a complete solipsist, the needs of family, partners, friends, employers, your own self and the world around you, all have to be juggled and balanced somehow or other. Belonging is complicated. Love is complicated. The creative life is a selfish one. On my office wall, I have a quote from the Ojibwe writer Louise Erdrich:

'*Life will break you. Nobody can protect you from that, and living alone won't either, for solitude will also break you with its yearning. You have to love. You have to feel. It is the reason you are here on earth. You are here to risk your heart. You are here to be swallowed up. And when it happens that you are broken, or betrayed, or left, or hurt, or death brushes near, let yourself sit by an apple tree and listen to the apples falling all around you in heaps, wasting their sweetness. Tell yourself you tasted as many as you could.*'

It's late evening by the time I walk up towards the shipwreck — more than an hour and a half's walk from Haida House. I sit and eat my cheese sandwiches on some driftwood at the edge of the dunes and I have what I can only describe as a 'prickly' moment. One of those moments when you feel very exposed, as if someone is watching you. It occurs to me that perhaps coming so far alone is not a good idea. The sun is descending behind the trees towards the invisible horizon. The beach is deserted. Supposing I have an accident? There's no mobile phone signal, no-one knows where I am. I shake it off and carry on with my

The Pesuta shipwreck, Tlell

trek. It takes longer than I anticipate to walk to the Pesuta — I can see the ribs of the ship sticking up out of the sand from quite a distance away, but it never seems to get any nearer. When I reach the mouth of the river the tide is already coming in and the water much too deep to walk across. I decide that, as I can't get to the shipwreck, I'd like to walk back to the motel down the river rather than retrace my footsteps along the beach. There are woods on either side, but there's a fringe of level bank that is walkable. As I turn round the end of the sandy spit there's a small movement about a hundred yards further down the river, something dark emerging from the water — a shadow that slips into the woods on the opposite bank. A deer, I think at first.

But, as I walk on down the river bank, I notice a line of prints coming from the direction of the dunes towards the edge of the river — large prints, single track, not running around as a dog would, but strolling purposefully on until they enter the water. There are big dints made by heavy paw pads with four claw marks on each foot deeply incised into the damp sand. Bear prints! It seems that he or she has been munching wild strawberries in the

205

dunes just behind the spot where I was eating my supper. Lucky for me that the bear didn't take a fancy to cheese sandwiches. Lucky for me that the black bears of Haida Gwaii are quite shy and prefer to avoid human contact. I decide to walk back to Haida House along the beach. There are bears in these woods and I might not be so lucky a second time.

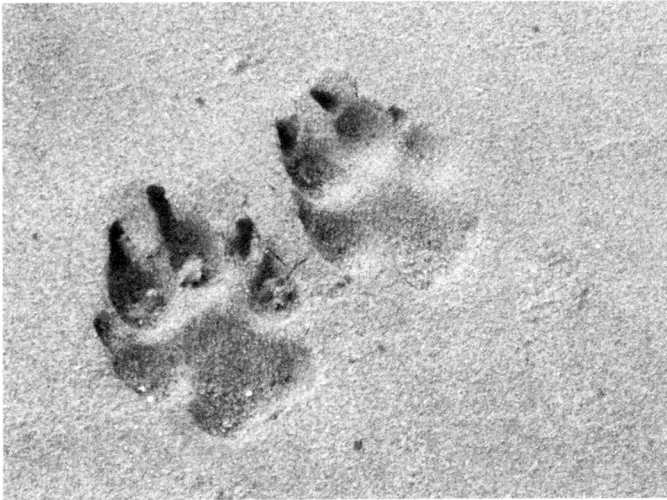

Black Bear paw prints

18. The Bank Robber's Wife

'In another life, this place was my home.
I feel the rising of a forgotten knowledge
like a spring from hidden aquifers under the earth.'
Susan Musgrave, 'The Sangan River Meditations'.[99]

I share my breakfast table with Ben, who is really interesting to talk to. He tells me there's a book I must read called *The Last Great Sea*, by Terry Glavin, which is about the natural history of the Pacific. Ben also talks about lighthouse keepers on the Hecate Strait and how one particular lighthouse up near Prince Rupert was chained to the rocks more than ninety feet above sea level. But in spite of its anchors, the lighthouse, its surrounding buildings, and its keepers were swept away in one memorable storm. Thirty metre waves are not unusual here.

After breakfast I drive up to Masset on a clear, gloriously sunny day arriving at Copper Beech in time for coffee. There's an air of spring-cleaning and discombobulation this morning. Susan is back and a plumber is taking apart the faucets in the bathroom and mending a small fountain in the garden. Elle is dashing about on errands.

An elderly man is sitting at the table on the terrace surrounded by stones. His name is Jim Roberts and he's a poet. He tells me he comes here regularly to find pebbles on the beach which he is now sorting into agates and jaspers and other semi-precious gems. The recent gales have brought in a good haul. He's trying to decide what to discard because, like me, he has to get the small plane back to Vancouver tomorrow and the weight allowance is critical. He shows me what whole agates look like. They are rather like geodes, a barrel shape of milky rock that looks as if it's coated in flour, but inside there's the glowing, translucent gold of the gemstone. Jim has collected some beautiful specimens and is finding it hard to choose between them.

We have coffee together and talk about poetry. Jim's last book was called, intriguingly, *From an argument I've taken with me*, but he tells me it's out of print and only available from second hand dealers at ridiculous prices that no one is going to pay. There's a book lying open on the table beside him. It's by a Canadian author, a follower of Noam Chomsky, called Stephen Pinker. Jim tells me that it's about how the mind creates language and how children instinctively use grammar — that grammar is integral to how our minds work, not simply a system imposed on our methods of communication. It's an instinctive logic. Jim makes it sound so good I write down the title to check later.

While we're talking about words Susan and the plumber and various other workmen come and go. There are snatches of gossip, a brief glimpse of the frustrations of living off the grid, the fact that the new washing machine still hasn't arrived, conversations about whirlpools in the ocean, and a third party who has been 'disrespecting someone else's property' by borrowing things and not bringing them back. I realise how hard it is for people in small communities to share limited space. If you fall out with someone there's nowhere to go.

Susan is just as she looks on the internet, but much more vivid. She is restless, always busy, her observations quite sharp. I've read Susan's poetry and own one of her collections. She connects with life head on, and it hasn't always been kind. We chat about poetry and life on Haida Gwaii and my bad timing. It's sad that there isn't time to get to know each other better. I know that Susan is a passionate advocate of knowing how to feed yourself from the land. She has a house near the Sangan River and does a lot of foraging. She also has a gun and knows how to hunt deer, skin them and prepare them from the cookpot. The experience has turned her into a fish-eating vegetarian. "Every time I looked at my plate I could see two brown eyes looking up at me." But she still thinks it's important that we know how to do it.

There's one subject we don't discuss. I imagine she must be quite tired of being asked about it. Several people here have told me about Susan's absent husband. "He's a good guy," people say. "Real nice". Stephen is out on licence after an 18 year prison sentence for bank robbery, living at a half-way house in Victoria, but due to come home shortly. According to a recent interview I read on the internet, Susan can't wait for normal life to resume. Stephen's story is like something out of a novel. He was a member of the infamous 'Stop-Watch Gang' who robbed more than a hundred banks in Canada and the USA during the seventies and eighties. Susan met him while he was serving a prison sentence for those offences. He had written a novel about his experiences, *Jackrabbit Parole*, which he sent to her. They married while he was still inside. He was released in 1987 on parole and went on to write a prize-winning collection of essays. Unfortunately, although Stephen was straight for over a decade, the drug habit that had led to his first encounter with the law drew him back into another bank heist in 1999. Now 65, Stephen has apparently put it all behind him and is looking forward to living quietly with Susan in Masset. To impoverished poets scraping a living all over the globe, the idea of someone pulling off bank heists to support their art might seem quite romantic, but the reality of being married to a convicted criminal is different. The strain and sadness of it is in Susan's poetry. So much of her marriage has been spent alone and in prison visiting.

Once I've unpacked and tucked myself back into what I've come to think of as 'my' room, I get in the car to take a last look at Old Massett and its totems. Each time I go there I find more of them to look at. And I look hard, knowing that this may be the last time I get to see them. On the way back I pay a visit to the maritime museum, which is in New Masset and documents the European history of the settlement. It's a small wooden bungalow in colonial style, full of the serendipity of the personal belongings, documents and domestic objects left behind by the settlers. There are also reminiscences written by the people themselves, though not all were literate. Many of them were from the highlands of Scotland, or farm labourers from England, lured by the thought of working their own land. Most were young and willing to work themselves to the bone for the chance to be their own bosses. Others came via the gold fields, once they had realised the unlikelihood of 'striking it rich' and that the true gold was in the forests and the waters of British Columbia.

It was a tough life, without the amenities they were used to in the west. The first doctor only arrived in Masset in 1909 with his wife, a trained nurse. They were medical missionaries aiming to treat the sick and convert the heathen. Their first hospital was a tent — destroyed when a tree fell on it in a storm. There's a photograph of Dr Allan Fraser, his wife and their five children posed in formal Edwardian costumes, totally inappropriate garments for either the environment or the weather.

The next physician Dr John Dunn arrived with his wife Lillian in 1921, but found the (European) population too healthy to support his family without the backing of a missionary fund. He had to become a hotelier, proprietor of the Queen's Hotel in Masset, because the medical practice didn't pay enough to keep them.

By 1923 there was also a dentist on Haida Gwaii, Dr Peter Size, whose wife Emily acted as his nurse. They had an itinerant practice and used to tour the islands on foot carrying all their instruments and the wheel to power the drill, staying for a few days in each place. But they made enough money to have a house in Queen Charlotte and another in Masset.

Their stories are told in a big file of memoirs and reminiscences, some of which have become published books, and there's a wonderful collection of photographs. I sit for a while thumbing through the files, fascinated by what they tell me of people's lives and the changing landscape of Haida Gwaii. A hundred years ago the road to Tow Hill is described in one memoir as 'a broken little trail stealing away into the woods.' In the early part of the twentieth century it led to a broken-down farmstead where the Carey brothers (Len and Austin from Barnstaple in Somerset) had lived since they came to the Charlottes from a failed farming venture on the Prairies. Mildred Valley Thornton, an artist who

210

came to Haida Gwaii intent on painting a vanishing society, described Len (the only one left alive when she met him) as 'a queer little piece of humanity', wizened, stooped and wearing a flat cap. Since his brother died, Len had become an artist, painting glass balls and making drawings of the landscape and wild life. He fed the deer and the wild geese and the grouse and the bears who came into his garden and were totally unafraid of him.

The house, as Mildred described it, was something else. He lived in one room, a cot bed in the corner, a rusting stove in the middle next to a chopping block, the floor ankle deep in wood chippings and sawdust and discarded clothing that lay where it had fallen from the pegs on the wall. There was no sign of any housekeeping, yet he seemed perfectly content. Mildred was horrified by the muddle, but appreciated that the old man had his eyes on higher things. Others thought that Len had 'gone native'.

The two brothers kept goats when they first came to Masset, but after a while could only bring themselves to sell the milk; as they became increasingly eccentric they couldn't bear to kill the goats. They had a horse but couldn't bear to make it work, so they dug their land by hand and went everywhere on foot. Len lived 'in closer and closer communion' with the creatures of the wild, painting in the evenings and during the day enjoying the wild landscape he felt he belonged to. Mildred observed that 'he was … one of the few completely happy persons I have ever known.'[100]

Two other 'characters', Charlie Spence and his wife Alice, feature in *Days on the North Beach 1939* by H.B. Phillips. Charlie was born in the Shetlands and emigrated to Canada in 1908. Although he had come as a gold prospector, his claim vanished under the ocean as Cape Fife, at the north of Haida Gwaii, was eroded by the sea. So he and his new wife, the niece of another claim-holder, tried to make a living farming the land, in circumstances as tough as the ones Charlie had left behind as a crofter. It was a family partnership. According to the records Alice 'worked as hard as any man'. There are photographs of her in tweed skirt and jacket, wrapped in a headscarf, up to her ankles in mud, in the middle of a ploughed field. But it was still difficult to make a living, and during the First World War, Alice and Charlie became lighthouse keepers. Farming proved much too hard on Haida Gwaii and the two main sources of income soon became fishing and logging. But nowhere in any of the memoirs is any acknowledgement of the fact that these claim-holders were settling on land that belonged to someone else.

The woman looking after the museum mentions the cemetery where many of these early settlers were 'put to rest'. I follow her instructions and drive up a small lane, easy to overlook, that turns off Tow Hill Road and winds up into the woods on the fringe of the Nature Reserve. Avoiding the potholes and beginning to wonder if I've come to the right place, I suddenly come upon a big lych gate incongruously in the middle of the forest, with no fence or wall on either side of it. I park the car and walk through. It's like no cemetery I've ever been to.

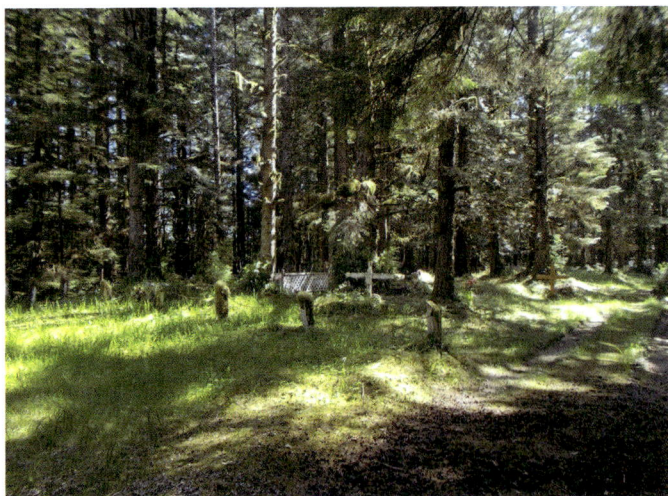

The old European cemetry, Masset

There's one fairly new grave — just a mound decorated with shells and pebbles, but most of the rest are simply shallow humps in the ground, covered in moss. The most recent are still marked with a wooden cross carved with the name of the occupant, but as I walk further and further into the trees, the crosses have all rotted away and the mounds are less and less distinguishable from the natural undulations of the forest floor, among the fallen tree trunks and leaf litter. The standing trees are close together, new saplings and older specimens with a flourishing undergrowth of what I've learned to recognise as thimble berry, bunch berry and dwarf dogwood. And under it all lie the ancient dead, the Len Careys and Alice Spences, all rotting peacefully down into the ground in a green dusk. It must be one of the most beautiful places in which to end your time on earth.

I'm invited out this evening. Elle is taking me to her friend Bella's home for dinner. Elle's daughter has come to Copper Beech for the summer season to help her so there are three of us, in an old American car, the size of a truck, with the springs gone, clutching a sack of brown rice and a chicken daubed in butter and fresh herbs. We bounce up the Tow Hill Road, to where the Carey brothers must once have lived and Charlie and Alice Spence. Bella lives in a cabin tucked into the woods near North Beach. It's a house she has built herself over twenty years, with a compost toilet, her own well water, photo-voltaic cells to run a few electrical appliances, a wood burner for winter heat. It doesn't cost much to live out there, particularly if you can provide most of your own food. Bella runs a summer business in Masset and has two children. Her son arrives while we're talking, having walked from the village, and there's a strange atmosphere of conflict. I open the bottle of wine I've brought and we drink it outside in the forest clearing while Elle cooks and Elle's daughter swings in a hammock reading a book. Bella says it's been hard living here. She loves it, but her husband didn't stay and her children would prefer to be somewhere more lively. They miss contact with the outside world and other kids.

For dinner we eat the spider crabs that Elle and Bella caught the day before, mopping up the juices with homemade bread. They tell me that the crabs are coming inshore to mate at the moment, so you can catch them easily, but you keep only the males, which have a thinner stomach on the underside — females are much broader. The crabs have been boiled, cooled and chopped in half. We eat the flesh straight out of the shell with garlic and lemon butter and a salad from her veggie bed out the back, wired over to protect it from the deer and the chickens. This is foraged food — free from the wild. How human beings originally lived.

Then we have Elle's chicken, which is a Mennonite chicken, huge and freshly killed, with chard and brown rice that has the juices of the chicken spooned over it. This is one of the best meals I've had since I arrived in Canada. I ask about the Mennonites and Bella tells me they have two communities here, just out of Masset going south. They farm and you can get chickens and short ribs and sausages and fresh strawberries and other produce from them. Their children aren't allowed to mix and the boys mustn't be in the same room alone with a girl or a woman, which sometimes makes things awkward.

After dinner we go outside and sit in the garden again. It feels very special, sitting there in the dusk, talking to Bella, Elle and her daughter about their lives. The boy won't join us, but sits on the sofa with his computer, deep in some teenage depression. We are all rather subdued — Bella because of her son, Elle because she's tired after a hard day, and me because it's my last night on Haida Gwaii.

As we drive back over the Sangan River, it's still a beautiful evening. We're far north and it will soon be the longest day. The sun has only just set and the sky is a fiery red with the afterglow of one of the sunsets that Haida Gwaii is famous for.

19. Everything is Connected

'They say if you live on an island for too long, you merge with it. Your bones become the sand, your blood the ocean ... No matter where you and your children travel, the island is home.'
Terri Janke, Butterfly Song, Torres Strait Islands, 2005

It's time to leave. I feel very emotional and full of sadness. There are only a few places in the world that feel like a spiritual home, but this is one of them, and a part of yourself always gets left behind — snagged on the barbed wire fence like sheep's wool. I'm leaving a lot of myself on Haida Gwaii, as well as people I want to keep as friends for life, but know that I may never see again.

I say goodbye to Elle and her daughter and promise to keep in touch. Susan Musgrave gives me an eagle feather and some precious eagle down that is supposed to make certain that I will come back. Then I load my luggage into the Dodge. I'm giving Jim Roberts a lift up to the airport this morning, as we're leaving on the same plane. The car hire office have given me instructions to leave the car in the airport car park with the key in the ignition; someone will pop up to collect it later. Where else in the world would returning a hire car be so casual?

There's only a small group in the airport building waiting for the plane. The flight is fairly empty so no-one is bothering to weigh the luggage. Jim needn't have worried about his collection of stones and I could have carried another couple of books. My clam shell is carefully packed into a plastic sandwich box with my feathers and my pebbles in bubble wrap. Everyone talks to everyone else while we're waiting, watching the cloud ceiling nervously, hoping it's not too low. One of the women tells me that she's here to meet some new arrivals and take them down to Queen Charlotte. She drove up from Vancouver a couple of days ago to provide transport services for tourist groups. The season is just getting underway. She tells me about her journey, which had taken almost five days because of flash floods that had wiped out the road in a couple of places.

On the plane — this time with earplugs to lessen the noise — I prepare for my last glimpse of Haida Gwaii, a forested, cloud-wreathed group of islands in a grey seascape, fading into the distance under the wing as we swerve across the Hecate Strait to follow the mainland coast south to Vancouver. Below us now are the coastal mountain ranges, not as spectacular as the Rockies, but still very impressive. From above we have a good view of the peaks and valleys and rocky ridges that seem to extend forever towards the horizon. I've been told that there is less snow on the

The retreating glaciers

mountains than at any other time in recorded history. Many of the peaks are naked rock, with the odd white patch in sheltered crevices. Recently, even in winter, the mountains haven't been white the way they usually are because of decreasing snowfalls. Because of the lack of snow-melt many of the rivers we're flying over are already dry. Canada, historically, has had more glaciers than almost any other country, but here the remaining glaciers, fish-boning their way into the valleys, have receded dramatically, and it's obvious even to someone who doesn't know the terrain.

There are dry, U-shaped valleys where, until recently, great rivers of ice scoured and polished the rock. You can see the smooth, high-tide lines between the established tree growth and the gritty surface of the remaining ice, many metres below, a rocky surface exposed too recently for any kind of plant to colonise. The glaciers are retreating fast, some of them now only a nose of dirty white at the top of the valley. In places there are emerald lakes where the last of the ice has melted high up on the mountain, creating a 'hanging lake'. There are also deep depressions at the top of some mountains, surrounded by a ridge on three sides, which should have been packed with snow and ice to feed a glacier. But now there is only a puddle of water, trickling out onto a gritty scree. Climate change and its consequences, are very obvious in Canada.

Now proficient at using Canadian transport systems I take a shuttle bus from the airport terminal to the Sky station. Although I have invitations from both my new friends I'm staying with Julia rather than Colette, because she lives in the most convenient place for me to get to the airport tomorrow. Her home is situated in one of the most beautiful areas of Vancouver, and I have a pleasant walk through tree-lined streets, passing some interesting examples of colonial architecture — including a baronial hall complete with tower, built by a nostalgic nineteenth century immigrant. Julia's home, when I reach it, is completely modern. It's a house designed and created by its owners. Julia is a designer, her husband a sculptor and their house is a work of art — the way the spaces open out into each other, the way the light falls into the building, the way internal and external space connect. Everything, down to the bath towels and bed linen, is personally designed to function exactly how the owners want to live. It could be pretentious, but it isn't. Just a really beautiful space that feels comfortable to live in and is also eco-friendly.

Julia's husband is away, so we go out for dinner to an Asian fusion restaurant nearby, where I eat tamarind and yogurt chicken, hot and sour, and feel very well fed. This diversity of food is one of the plus factors of living in a city with so many different cultures. Julia gives me quite a lot of information about Vancouver while we eat, and, as I guessed, the city is really a series of villages and you have to know where to go. Afterwards, Julia drives me round some beautiful, and exclusive, areas where there are beaches and tens of kilometers of waterside walks with views across to the mountains. Houses in this area sell for more than five million dollars. Julia also gives me a list of galleries that specialise in contemporary aboriginal art, most of them in one particular street within walking distance of the house.

After a nightcap, and checking in online for my flight tomorrow, I sleep blissfully in the guest bed. In the morning after a leisurely breakfast, I walk down the hill to the South Granville area of Vancouver which has lovely views across the centre of the city, to the harbour area and the mountains beyond. It's an interesting district, with a lot of original art deco buildings, little boutiques, patisseries and coffee shops. There are several galleries I've come to visit, but one in particular has a big recommendation.

The Douglas Reynolds Gallery is small, but has a large collection of contemporary indigenous art beautifully displayed. There are pieces by Jim Hart and Robert Davidson, whose work I've come to see. Both artists were trained in the Haida tradition, following their ancestor Charles Edenshaw — Jim Hart is now Chief Edenshaw and pays tribute to his predecessor; 'His pieces all carry this: the respect of his people, the respect of his ancestors, the respect of his family. Charles is part of Haida Hierarchy.' The Haida language, like most First Nation languages, has no word for art, just as it has no word for nature, because art can't be separated from their everyday lives. It is an integral part of their being and this wholeness is sometimes referred to as the 'Haida Way'. Take away the people, Bill Reid wrote, and you would have only 'empty images', true to the formal rules of art but 'without any emotion behind them.' Reid believed, passionately, that 'great art must be a living thing,/or it is not art at all.'[101] It is essential that the skills and the cultural knowledge are passed on from one generation to another. Of the younger generations inheriting this tradition, Jim Hart writes: 'we must carry on, in the Haida Way. We owe it to our ancestors who created and left us this Grand Legacy of high Art, our History. We owe it to our future generations to fuel them to carry on with pride and dignity.'[102]

But a living art must also develop. Robert Davidson, also Charles Edenshaw's great grandson, says that 'the magic of Edenshaw's work embodies millennia of development of Haida art'. And now that tradition of Haida art is being taken forward into the twenty-first century, with the use of new tools and materials and the influence of new ideas. It's impossible for both traditional and imported art forms to have existed side by side for nearly two centuries without some influence from one to the other. Robert Davidson says he can see a definite progression in the development of Haida art over the last two hundred years and, 'who knows where the art will go from here? The limitation is really up the artist in the present moment'.[103]

There are some stunning modern pieces in the gallery. There's a beautiful Raven sculpture by Jim Hart and two red metal Ravens by Robert Davidson, but the ones that really catch my imagination are pieces from artists I haven't previously encountered. One is called 'Moon' by a Salish artist, Tom Eneas. It's a circular wall plaque, carved from red cedar, with Raven at its centre, peering from the face of the moon. And then I turn a corner and find myself face to face with Marcus Alfred's D'Zonoqua. The black mask is taller than me, with a big gaping mouth, hollow eyes and black hair. The sudden impact is profound and defies logic. It is so beautiful and so terrifying at the same time, that I'm taken aback. It comes as a reminder. The wild woman inside me is, indeed, a thing to be afraid of. If I really let go, what wouldn't I be capable of?

Too soon it's time to go. I have to say goodbye to Julia and her family, to Vancouver, and to British Columbia. There hasn't been enough time to see everything I want to see, or meet everyone I would like to talk to. I feel quite miserable as I climb out of the shuttle bus with my luggage and walk into the airport for the last time.

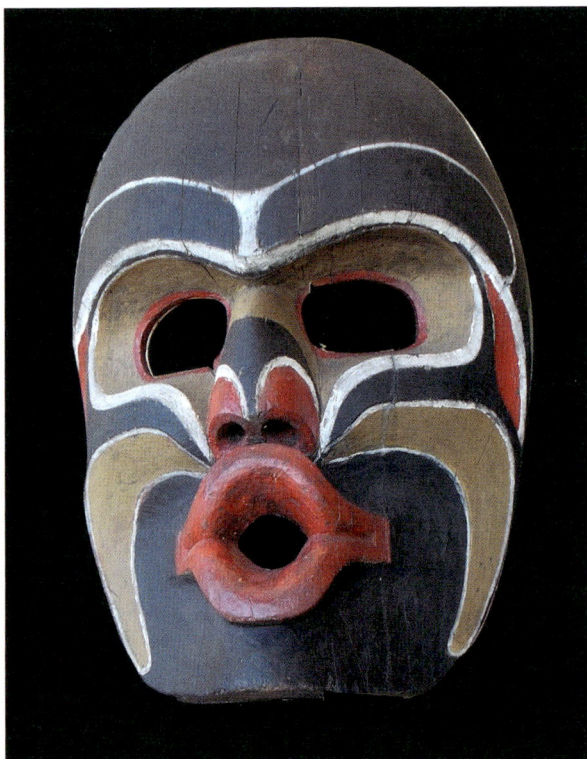

D'Sonoqua mask, Museum of Anthropology, Vancouver

In the departure lounge is a sculpture that tells the story of Fog Woman and the Raven, carved by Dempsey Bob, another artist new to me. In the story, Raven pretended to love Fog Woman, but only married her for the salmon she brought with her. Fog Woman is carved with salmon in her hair as well as in her hands. Raven became wealthy from the huge salmon harvests, began to take his wife for granted and finally to mistreat her. So Fog Woman left him and she took the salmon with her. Raven realised his mistake but it was too late, his wife had already evaporated back into coastal fog. However, Fog Woman didn't want the ordinary people to suffer just because of Raven's selfish greed, so every spring she arranged for the salmon to return to the rivers for a brief period so that they could feed on them.

This is definitely a parable for our time. When I look at the carvings I think about the rivers in British Columbia where the salmon no longer return, or arrive in very small numbers only one year in three. I think about the First Nation blockade of the fish farms, and the Kayak protests against arctic drilling operations. You can't take the natural world for granted — it has to be nurtured or, like Fog Woman, it will evaporate with all its rich resources. 'Haida culture is not simply song and dance,' Guujaaw writes in a poem. 'It is about being confronted by the great storms of winter/and trying to look after this precious place'. [104]

My modest hold-all (the small airplanes don't like suitcases) hardly makes a dent in my gigantic transatlantic luggage allowance. I've survived four weeks with only a couple of T-shirts, three pairs of trousers, four pairs of knickers and a few fleecy tops, plus a pair of walking boots, a pair of trainers and a pair of sandals. At home I have cupboards full of clothes — smart clothes, knocking around clothes, outdoor activity clothes, summer clothes, spring and fall clothes, winter clothes. And shelves of shoes to match any eventuality and any outfit. When I was a child, in post-war austerity, we had one set of 'good' clothes, our school uniform and one set of weekend scruffy stuff for doing what children do. My grandmother would buy me a new 'best' outfit every Easter, but it was the only new one I'd get all year. Once, an aunt, who lived in America, bought me a party dress from a Sears catalogue for my Christmas present. I've remembered that dress all my life. Footwear was in short supply too. We only had two pairs of shoes all year — sandals in summer and Clarks' brogues in winter — and a pair of Wellingtons. During the summer we might also have a pair of cheap canvas shoes which were called 'sandshoes' or 'daps'. There was a lot of handing down of clothes and shoes. One of my aunts was very skilled in making alterations. No one had much money in the forties and fifties and, after the war, the real cost of buying materials, making things and transporting them had to be paid. Now, my grandchildren have cupboards stuffed with colourful outfits. Why not, when clothes cost so little and you can pick them up at the supermarket? A pair of children's play shoes cost only slightly more than a five litre container of milk. How this can happen is a mystery to most of us and we don't question it because we're just glad to have the opportunity to possess things at ridiculous prices.

Finally the departure board lights up and it's time to go. It's a night flight and, thanks to a large glass of wine and the number of miles I've walked on Vancouver pavements today, I sleep very well and wake up in another country, another culture.

Heathrow is a shock. It is crowded, bad tempered, there are armed police everywhere and passengers coming off the plane are herded here and there like animals. I find myself being penned up in a corridor with hundreds of others with no explanation and the clock ticking for my flight connection. The rules have been changed while I was away. It seems that, even though we are 'in transit', we have to go through a security check and passport inspection. The computers are down and they have to do it manually. I plead my connecting flight and kind passengers allow me to go to the head of the queue. I race through only to find myself penned in another queue, this time for an electronic security check. Outer clothing removed, laptop and Kindle extracted from bags, I get to the machine eventually, only to be singled out for closer inspection. The small cans of maple syrup I bought in the airport as souvenirs for my children can't be allowed through, even though they are in sealed bags, bought in duty free. Pointless to argue that I haven't been anywhere since I went through security in Vancouver. I barely make my connecting flight.

Several hours later, after another airport arrival and a long train journey, I'm back home. It's depressing; the pile of mail on the dining table, neatly sorted by my kind neighbour; a cold house, smelling of damp and neglect. It's echoingly empty. I turn on the television for company. People are killing each other in the Middle East, people are drowning in the Mediterranean, governments are arguing about the economic figures, there's another corruption scandal, and our own government has just proposed a law making fracking legal without any community consultation whatsoever. They're nitpicking on whether desperate people fleeing war and starvation are refugees or economic migrants. A month away and the world looks the same. But has anything changed? Have I changed?

I look out of the window at the river and the lush burgeoning green of early English summer. Cow parsley and Dames' Violet are waist high on the river bank and the heron is standing on one leg, looking hopefully at the water above the weir. It feels very peaceful. I realise that something has changed for me. The First Nation people have given me Hope, only a glimmer, like a glowing fragment of coal on a dark winter night. And I know now what is the most important thing. This earth connection, this great calm that comes from being consciously part of the natural world and its rich cycle of birth, death and everything in between. It's very simple; when people's survival depends on the environment around them, they take care of it. If you break that link, people don't and everything suffers. We have to re-make that connection.

What I've learned in Haida Gwaii, from the Haida people fighting for their environment, has also made me realise that the planet doesn't need me to find peace of mind and body — that selfish equilibrium that would mean turning my attention off from all the troubling things of everyday, the economic and climatic threats, the human and environmental tragedies — the world needs me to be angry — to go out spitting and fighting for its own equilibrium — the natural balance that has been disturbed. The world does not need me to be peaceful. Escape is not the answer; it is another form of denial. Because Wild, if it is the soul of the world, is neither peaceful nor benign. It is beautiful — so beautiful it makes your bones ache — it is also brutal, fertile and ferocious and there is something of it in all of us. As Raven said, 'I am this, and I am that too.' We are part of it.

I know I have to stop travelling so much, stop buying so much, and that I have to begin to be more active in the attempt to prevent our planet being trashed by a heedless, uncaring consumer/capitalist culture. I live in a democracy, and I have to be aware and to take ownership of what the government does in my name. Neglecting to do that allows things like the cultural genocide in British Columbia to happen. This is my planet, my responsibility, my life. Okay, so maybe one person can't change the world, one person can't challenge a global corporation that has grown into a monster. But if one person doesn't start to try, then no one else is ever going to do it and there are a lot of people out there who feel the same. Alone, I'm nothing. Together we can all make a difference. As the Haida say, 'Everything is connected'.[105]

Select Bibliography

BRINGHURST, ROBERT, *A Story as Sharp as a Knife*, 2ⁿᵈ Edition, Douglas & McIntyre, Vancouver, 2011.

BRINGHURST, ROBERT, *Nine Visits to Myth World*, Douglas & McIntyre, Vancouver, 2001.

BRINGHURST, ROBERT, *The Tree of Memory*, Counterpoint Press, Berkeley, 2008.

BUTCHER, MARGARET, *The Letters of Margaret Butcher*, ed. Mary Ellen Kelm, University of Calgary Press, Calgary, 2006.

CARMICHAEL, ALFRED, *Indian Legends of Vancouver Island*, The Musson Book Company Ltd., Toronto, 1922, Illus. J. Semeyn.

CARR, EMILY, *Hundreds and Thousands*, Douglas & McIntyre, Vancouver, 2006.

CARR, EMILY, *Klee Wyck*, Oxford University Press, Toronto, 1941.

CHARLES EDENSHAW, Catalogue, ed. Robin K. Wright & Daina Augaitis, Black Dog Publishing, London, 2013

CHAMBERLIN, J.EDWARD, *If This is Your Land, Where are Your Stories?*, Vintage, Canada, 2004.

COLLISON, W.H., *In the Wake of the War Canoe*, The Musson Book Co., Toronto, 1915.

DAVIDSON, FLORENCE EDENSHAW, *During My Time: A Haida Woman*, ed. Margaret B. Blackman, Douglas & McIntyre Ltd, Vancouver, 1985

From the Forest to the Sea: Emily Carr in British Columbia, Catalogue, ed. Sarah Milroy & Ian Dejardin, Art Gallery of Ontario, Toronto, 2014.Gill, Ian, *All That We Say Is Ours*, p.42, Douglas & McIntyre, Vancouver, 2009.

GLAVIN, TERRY, *The Last Great Sea*, Greystone Books, Vancouver, 2000.

HARE, JAN, AND BARMAN, JEAN, *Good Intentions Gone Awry; Emma Crosby and the Methodist Mission on the Northwest Coast*, University of British Columbia, Vancouver, 2006.

Haida Gwaii: Human History & Environment, ed by Daryl W. Fedje and Rolf W. Mathewes

HOARE, PHILIP, *Leviathan*, Fourth Estate, London, 2009.

JAMIE, KATHLEEN, *Findings*, Sort of Books, London, 2005.

JAMIE, KATHLEEN, *Sightlines*, Sort of Books, London, 20012.

JEFFRIES, RICHARD, *The Story of my Heart*, Longmans Green & Co., London, 1883.

KLEIN, NAOMI, *This Changes Everything*, Penguin, London, 2015.

KNIGHT, EMMA LOUISE, *The Kwakwaka'wakw Potlatch Collection and its Many Social Contexts: Constructing a Collection's Object Biography*, University of Toronto, 2013, https://tspace. library.utoronto.ca/bitstream/1807/42997/1/Knight_Emma_L_ 201311_Mmst_thesis.pdf accessed 13th July, 2015

MACFARLANE, ROBERT, *The Wild Places,* Granta Books, London, 2008.

Raven Travelling: Two Centuries of Haida Art, Douglas & McIntyre, Vancouver, 2006.

REID, WILLIAM, AND BRINGHURST, ROBERT, *Raven Steals the Light*, Douglas & McIntyre, Vancouver, 1996.

SAID, EDWARD, *Culture and Imperialism*, Vintage, London, 1994.

SAID, EDWARD, *Reflections on Exile,* Granta Books, London, 2001.

SEWID, JAMES, *Guests Never Leave Hungry*, ed. James P.

SPRADLEY, MCGILL, Queen's University Press, Montreal, 1972.

THORNTON, MILDRED VALLEY, *Potlatch People*, Hancock House Publishers Ltd, Surrey, B.C., 1966.

VALLIANT, JOHN, *The Golden Spruce*, Arrow Books, London, 2007.

VREELAND, SUSAN, *The Forest Lover*, Penguin, London, 2004.

Articles and Papers, news items, tv and radio programmes
Be Brave - come together - http://www.filmsforaction.org/takeaction/five-ways-of-being-that-can-change-the-world/
First Peoples' Heritage, Language, and Culture Council, Report

on the Status of B.C. First Nations Languages, (Brentwood Bay, B.C.: First Peoples' Heritage, Language, and Culture Council, 2010).

Canada, Towards a New Beginning: A Foundational Report for a Strategy to Revitalize First Nation, Inuit, and M — tis Languages and Cultures, Task Force on Aboriginal Languages and Cultures (Ottawa: Department of Canadian Heritage, 2005), 33.

'Holding Our Tongues.' ABC Radio National. http://www.abc.net.au/rn/awaye/stories/2010/2758510.htm

The 8th Fire, documentary, CBC Illustrations

End Notes

1.http://www.theecologist.org/Interviews/2843602/the_american_genocide_indigenous_resistance_and_human_survival_roxanne_dunbarortiz.html

2. Her English name was Agnes Russ and her story is told by her gt-granddaughter, Marianne Jones, in the catalogue of an exhibition at Vancouver Art Gallery. *Raven Travelling: Two Centuries of Haida Art*, Douglas & McIntyre, Vancouver, 2008.

3.http://www.theglobeandmail.com/report-on-business/rob-magazine/clarence-louie-feature/article18913980/

4. http://susanpoint.com/

5. Carr, Emily, Growing Pains,

6. Carr, Emily, Hundreds and Thousands, June 17th, 1931, p.54

7. Carr, Emily, Hundreds and Thousands

8. First Nation Elder, quoted in the film The Winds of Heaven.

9. Edward Said, Cultural Imperialism,

10. Harmand, Jules, Domination et Colonisation, 1910, Flammarion

11. Dombey and Son, 1848, rprt. Harmondsworth, Penguin 1970 p. 50.

12. Naomi Klein, This Changes Everything, p.27

13. First Peoples' Heritage, Language, and Culture Council, Report on the Status of B.C. First Nations Languages, (Brentwood Bay, B.C.: First Peoples' Heritage, Language, and Culture Council, 2010).

14. 'Holding Our Tongues.' ABC Radio National. http://www.abc.net.au/rn/awaye/stories/2010/2758510.htm (accessed July 7th, 2015).

15. Mary Lou Fox, Ojibwe elder

16. First Peoples' Heritage, Language, and Culture Coun-

cil, Report on the Status of B.C. First Nations Languages, (Brentwood Bay, B.C.: First Peoples' Heritage, Language, and Culture Council, 2010).

17. First Peoples' Heritage, Language, and Culture Council, Report on the Status of B.C. First Nations Languages, (Brentwood Bay, B.C.: First Peoples' Heritage, Language, and Culture Council, 2010).

18. http://aeon.co/magazine/psychology/how-childhood-biography-shapes-adult-biology/

19. http://www.huffingtonpost.ca/2014/07/27/residential-school-survivors_n_5624586.html

20. https://www.aadnc-aandc.gc.ca/eng/1100100015644/1100100015649

21. http://www.firstnations.de/img/04-2-1-diorama-b.jpg

22. Griffin, Kevin (June 7, 2008). 'St. Michael's Residential School at Alert Bay'. Vancouver Sun. Accessed 11ᵗʰ July, 2015.

23. http://www.campbellrivermirror.com/news/291757931.html February 12ᵗʰ 2015, accessed 11ᵗʰ July 2015

24. Grandmother Agnes Alfred, Community Leader, Alert Bay

25. Knight, Emma Louise, *The Kwakwaka'wakw Potlatch Collection and its Many Social Contexts: Constructing a Collection's Object Biography*, University of Toronto, 2013

26. The Letters of Margaret Butcher, [January 1ˢᵗ, 1918] ed. Mary Ellen Kelm, University of Calgary Press, Calgary, 2006.

27. Knight, Emma Louise, *The Kwakwaka'wakw Potlatch Collection and its Many Social Contexts: Constructing a Collection's Object Biography*, University of Toronto, 2013

28. Margaret Blackman, Haida Traditional Culture, 'Swanton, Boas and the New Haida Sculpture'.

29. Knight, Emma Louise, *The Kwakwaka'wakw Potlatch Collection and its Many Social Contexts: Constructing a Collection's Object Biography*, University of Toronto, 2013

30. Pitt Rivers,'On the principles of classification adopted in the arrangement of his anthropological collection now exhibited in the Bethnal Green Museum.' JAI 4 [1874] 293-308

31. Knight, Emma Louise, *The Kwakwaka'wakw Potlatch Collection and its Many Social Contexts: Constructing a Collection's*

Object Biography, University of Toronto, 2013

32. Wedidi Speck, Hereditary Chief, Kwaigu'i First Nation, Museum of Anthropology, Vancouver, BC

33. Royal Commission on Indian Affairs, (McKenna-McBride Commission) *Report*, Vol 3, 1916

34. Hare, Jan, and Barman, Jean, Good Intentions Gone Awry, University of British Columbia, Vancouver, 2006.

35. The Letters of Margaret Butcher, [September 29th, 1916] ed. Mary Ellen Kelm, University of Calgary Press, Calgary, 2006.

36. The Letters of Margaret Butcher, [May 26th, 1917] ed. Mary Ellen Kelm, University of Calgary Press, Calgary, 2006.

37. The Letters of Margaret Butcher, [June 9th, 1918] ed. Mary Ellen Kelm, University of Calgary Press, Calgary, 2006.

38. The Letters of Margaret Butcher, [May 18th, 1919] ed. Mary Ellen Kelm, University of Calgary Press, Calgary, 2006.

39. The Letters of Margaret Butcher, [May 18th, 1919] ed. Mary Ellen Kelm, University of Calgary Press, Calgary, 2006.

40. The Letters of Margaret Butcher, [May 18th, 1919] ed. Mary Ellen Kelm, University of Calgary Press, Calgary, 2006.

41. Kilian, Christian, 'Mothers of a Native Hell', The Tyee, 2007

42. Carr, Emily, *Klee Wyck*, Chapter 6: D'Sonoqua,

43. Namgis Treaty News, 2003.

44. Alert Bay Community Report 2006: Adapting to Uncertain Futures.

45. http://www.firstnations.de/fisheries/kwakwakawakw-namgis.htm accessed 16th July 2015

46. Gill, Ian, *All That We Say Is Ours*, p.15, Douglas & McIntyre, Vancouver, 2009.

47. Perry Bellegarde, CBC News, 1st June, 2015, http://www.cbc.ca/news/aboriginal/perry-bellegarde-afn-chief-says-reconciliation-means-closing-poverty-gap-1.3095407

48. Tania Major, Kokoberra People, 2010, British Museum, Indigenous Australia, 2015.

49. Gill, Ian, *All That We Say Is Ours,* p.42, Douglas & McIntyre, Vancouver, 2009.

50. Stocker, Ralph, *Haida Gwaii Observer*, Friday May 29th 2015.

51. Sarton, May, *Journal of a Solitude*, September 17th and

18th, W.W. Norton & Co., 1993.
52. Daniel Swain, meteorologist, Stanford University.
53. Living Planet Report, WWF & Zoological Society of London http://www.theguardian.com/environment/2014/sep/29/earth-lost-50-wildlife-in-40-years-wwf [accessed 23rd August, 2015],
54. Stoknes, Per Espen, http://www.commondreams.org/views/2015/05/14/great-grief-how-cope-losing-our-world
55. Bringhurst, Robert, 'Wild Language', *The Tree of Meaning*, Counterpoint Press, Berkeley, 2008.
56.Yahgulanaas, Michael Nicoll, quoted in Gill, Ian, *All That We Say Is Ours*,
57. Dawson, George M., *Report on the Queen Charlotte Islands*, 1878
58. Davidson, Florence Edenshaw, *During My Time: A Haida Woman*, ed. Margaret B. Blackman, Douglas & McIntyre Ltd, Vancouver, 1985.
59. Marika Wilbur, Guardian 8th September, 2015. '*One woman's Mission to Photograph Every Native American Tribe in the US*'.
60. *Saturday Night Magazine*, Nov. 23, 1907, quoted in the Truth and Reconciliation Commission Report, June 2015. http://www.cbc.ca/news/aboriginal/truth-and-reconciliation-commission-by-the-numbers-1.3096185
61. Duncan Campbell Scott, deputy superintendent-general of Indian Affairs, 1913.
62. http://www.cbc.ca/news/aboriginal/truth-and-reconciliation-commission-by-the-numbers-1.3096185
63. *The Letters of Margaret Butcher,* [July 20th, 1919] ed. Mary Ellen Kelm, University of Calgary Press, Calgary, 2006.
64. http://www.wordswithjam.co.uk/2015/07/diversity-pt-1-come-on-guys-youve-had.html
65. Carmichael, Alfred, *Indian Legends of Vancouver Island*, p.7, The Musson Book Co., Toronto, 1922.
66. Carmichael, Alfred, *Indian Legends of Vancouver Island*, p.5, The Musson Book Co., Toronto, 1922.
67. 'As I have never heard anything further from the Haida Nation, I presume that my travel journal doesn't need permission'

68. https://haidanation.wordpress.com/2015/08/25/a-surreal-find/

69. Vaillant, John, *The Golden Spruce*, p.195, Arrow Books, London, 2007

70. http://pacificwild.org/search/content/enbridge

71. Gill, Ian, *All That We Say Is Ours*, pp. 167-8

72. *Haida Land Use Vision*, Council of the Haida Nation, 2005.

73. Gill, Ian, *All That We Say Is Ours*, p.128

74. Fedje, Daryl W., and Mathewes, Rolf W., ed. *Haida Gwaii: Human History & Environment*, foreword by Guujaaw.

75. Chamberlin, J. Edward, *If This is Your Land, Where are Your Stories?*, Vintage Books, Canada, 2004.

76. Kroeber, Alfred L., *Seven Mohave Myths,* transcriptions of the poet Pamich, University of California Press, 1948

77. Gill, Ian, *All That We Say Is Ours*, p120

78. http://www.canadiangeographic.ca/magazine/ma07/in-depth/

79. Valliant, John, *The Golden Spruce*, Arrow Books, London, 2007.

80. http://www.queen-charlotte-islands-bc.com/travel_guide/6_golden_spruce_white_raven.php

81. John R. Swanton to Franz Boas, 30th September, 1900, Archives, Dept of Anthropology, American Museum of Natural History, New York.

82. John R. Swanton to Walter I. Swanton, 21st October 1900, Swanton Family Papers, Schlesinger Library, Radcliffe Institute, Harvard University.

83. Bringhurst, Robert, *A Story as Sharp as a Knife*, p.71, 2nd Edition, Douglas & McIntyre, Vancouver, 2011.

84. Swanton, John R., *Emanuel Swedenborg: Prophet of the Higher Evolution,* The New Church Press, 1928.

85. Bringhurst, Robert, *A Story as Sharp as a Knife*, p.71, 2nd Edition, Douglas & McIntyre, Vancouver, 2011.

86. John R. Swanton to Franz Boas, 14th October, 1900, Archives, Dept of Anthropology, American Museum of Natural History, New York.

87. Bringhurst, Robert, *A Story as Sharp as a Knife*, p.227, 2nd Edition, Douglas & McIntyre, Vancouver, 2011.

88. John R. Swanton to Walter I. Swanton, 21st October 1900, Swanton Family Papers, Schlesinger Library, Radcliffe Institute, Harvard University.

89. John R. Swanton to Franz Boas, 16th January, 1901, Archives, Dept of Anthropology, American Museum of Natural History, New York.

90. Bringhurst, Robert, *A Story as Sharp as a Knife*, p.167, 2nd Edition, Douglas & McIntyre, Vancouver, 2011.

91. https://www.sfu.ca/brc/virtual_village/haida/skidegate/monumental-art-of-skidegate.html#Skidegate1A

92. Christopher Herndon, president and co-founder of conservation group Acaté, http://news.mongabay.com/2015/0624-hance-matses-encyclopedia.html#ixzz3eLU5V2vS

93. Lewis Collison, Chief Skidegate, 1966. Haida Heritage Centre Display.

94. Preamble to the Haida Constitution. Haida Heritage Centre.

95. Collison, W.H., *In the Wake of the War Canoe*, p.89, The Musson Book Co., Toronto, 1915.

96. Frame, Janet, *The Envoy From Mirror City*, RHNZ Vintage, New Zealand, 2000. (First published 1985)

97. Said, Edward, *Out of Place*, Granta Books, London, 2000.

98. *The Letters of Katherine Mansfield*, ed. Vincent O'Sullivan and Margaret Scott, Vol.V, to Sarah G. Millin, March 1922.

99. Musgrave, Susan, 'Spring', The Sangan River Meditations, *Origami Dove*, McClelland & Stewart, Toronto, 2011.

100. Thornton, Mildred Valley, *Potlatch People*, pp.71-3, Hancock House Publishers, Surrey, BC, 1966.

101. Nika Collison, and Bill Reid quoted in *Raven Travelling*, Douglas & McIntyre, Vancouver, 2006.

102. James Hart, Chief's Foreword, *Charles Edenshaw*, ed. Robin K. Wright & Daina Augaitis, Black Dog Publishing, London, 2013.

103. Robert Davidson, *Charles Edenshaw*, ed. Robin K. Wright & Daina Augaitis, Black Dog Publishing, London, 2013. Also *Raven Travelling: Two Centuries of Haida Art*, Douglas & McIntyre, Vancouver, 2006.

104. Guujaaw, *Raven Travelling: Two Centuries of Haida Art*, Douglas & McIntyre, Vancouver, 2006.
105. 'Be Brave - Come Together' http://www.filmsforaction.org/takeaction/five-ways-of-being-that-can-change-the-world/

28458460R00131

Printed in Great Britain
by Amazon